MW01620435

THE CURIOUS APE

BY SEAN STUART

First published in Sydney, Australia by Sean Stuart.
Copyright © 2020 by Sean Stuart. All Rights reserved.

The moral rights of the author have been asserted.

No part of this book may be used or reproduced in any matter whatsoever without written permission except in the case of brief quotations embodied in critical articles and reviews.

The information within this book is strictly for educational purposes. The book is not intended to be a substitute for the medical, legal or pastoral advice of licensed professionals. If you wish to apply ideas contained herein, you are taking full responsibility for your actions.

For business inquires contact the author at book@seanstuartcuriousape.com

Design by Studio 3:AM
Edited by Harriet Richert

To Joe and Jamie
for paving the path of disruption

CONTENTS

CATEGORIES

ATHLETE
PSYCHOLOGIST
INVESTIGATIVE JOURNALIST
SCIENTIST
PHILOSOPHER
WHISTLEBLOWER

INTRODUCTION

The Great Library of Alexandria was one of the largest and most important libraries of the ancient world. It held the works of some of the finest scholars of its day. There were works of literary mastery, and scrolls from the world's first mathematicians and astronomers. The library was believed to hold over 40,000 scrolls with some estimates as high as 400,000. It was an ancient database of ideas.

The library was accidentally burnt down by Julius Caesar in 48 B.C. A wealth of information incinerated into ash. One can only wonder where civilization would be if that library had not burnt down. What secrets of that time were lost?

The Joe Rogan podcast is probably the last thing that comes to mind when someone mentions the Library of Alexandria. How could a 21st century comedian who smokes copious amounts of pot be compared to an ancient historical monument? The comedian, mixed martial arts commentator and the former host of Fear Factor has created something of equal value in my opinion. He has created an online platform for some of our time's finest minds from Elon Musk to Sir Roger Penrose. It is a vast collection of long-form conversations featuring people whose ideas are responsible for shaping the foundations of our culture. From arts to politics to science, the podcast is a database of ideas. A public library.

This library is in danger not from a fire but a simple click. All it would take is an order from a suit in Silicon Valley and all the ideas and discussions would be effaced from the internet forever. The value that comes from these discussions is too great to be left solely in the YouTube or Spotify archive. History cannot repeat itself. The podcast contains ideas that need to be written. The podcast contains ideas that need to be shared.

This book condenses over 5,000 hours of podcasts and over thirty books into the most potent twenty-five ideas. These ideas cover topics from quantum mechanics, artificial intelligence and sex, to psychedelics and stoicism. The Curious Ape is an exploration of the best ideas from scientists, philosophers, psychologists, investigative journalists, athletes and even whistleblowers. There are ideas about living longer, being healthier, being happier, pushing harder and expanding consciousness. This might sound like a bad infomercial you hear in a motel room advertising a penis enlarger, but fear not, this book is about science, logic and reason. If you ever find yourself wondering are we are in a simulation, is there another version of yourself somewhere or are there lost ancient civilizations, then this book contains answers from leading experts in the field. The only disclaimer I will make is that if you are not inherently curious, this book is not for you. If you accept things the way they are, don't like debate or are not interested in why mushrooms could save the planet, you should probably stop reading. The ideas that lie within this book require an open mind but also a skeptical one. There are twenty one pages of references with every statistic, argument and idea supported by evidence. Please feel free to corroborate if your bullshit detector is going off, some things might seem hard to believe but they are none the less true. And now, before we go any further, how did a comedian from Los Angeles build one of the greatest public libraries of our time?

The year is 2008. Anderson Cooper stares stridently into the camera. He looks like a military commander deployed to the comfort of the CNN newsroom. His familiar voice elicits trust as he asks President Barack Obama to define patriotism. Millions of Americans sit fixated on the television. Every pixel on the screen is in the same configuration from houses in Louisiana to mansions in the Hamptons.

The next morning you can read about it in the papers. The New York Times says something pretentious like, "Obama's confident resolve proves incorrigible." While Fox News says something along the lines of, "Where is his birth certificate?" Late night talk show hosts make the same jokes to packed audiences instructed to do one thing, applaud.

Facebook comment sections become the battleground for cyber warfare as geriatrics with profile pictures of cats argue with people they will never meet.

Every conceivable insult will be made. Every conspiracy will be told. Your mother is a whore. Obama is an alien.

It is no secret America was divided in 2008. It still is. The division seems to extend to every part of the world like tectonic plates dividing continents in half. Him or her. Christian or atheist. Oppressor or victim. In the age of information distinctions between these categories have not become nuanced; they have become oversimplified. It seems understandable when you consider that humans have evolved over 200,000 years into a species with the ability for an individual to meaningfully engage in social groups of around only a hundred people. The internet has overwhelmed us with millions of divergent opinions and our brains can't keep up. We seek the shelter of online communities who think the same as us. Division deepens. The warmth of these echo-chambers keeps the winds of dissent away and toxic ideas grow as reasonable discussion is locked out. Facebook feeds are carefully cultivated to show us only what we want to see. The New York Times. Fox News. Pick a side or the tech giants will use their algorithms to do it for you. Hundreds of clickbait titles designed to keep you clicking with little regard for accuracy of reporting.

Mainstream media tries to package everything into ten-second video clips that will go viral on the internet. Experts are asked questions which they must answer with yes or no. It seems executives believe that viewers have the patience of a seven-year-old with ADHD.

In the summer of 2009, something changed. The Joe Rogan Experience began. Hosted by the comedian, Joe Rogan, the podcast was streamed on an appallingly low number of pixels, attracting about a hundred viewers. In the first podcast, stoned out of his mind, Rogan held what was to be over two hours of discussion with friend Brian Redban. The discussion ranged from why chimpanzees hadn't taken over the world to the nature of the solar system. No one could have told you then, but these high comedians were going to revolutionize mainstream media. In true counterculture spirit, the billion-dollar media empires were about to be outdone by a couple of dudes smoking a joint.

In 2019, the podcast had 190 million downloads a month. That means each episode is viewed by more people than all cable network channels. In 2020, Spotify purchased the licensing rights of the podcast for over US$100 million. The podcast is a cultural phenomenon. Presidential candidates including

Bernie Sanders used the platform to reach millions of young people. Perhaps what best encapsulates the podcast's impact is when Elon Musk smoked a joint on the show causing a 4 percent drop in the Tesla stock price the next day. The corporate world was taking notice but the podcast's impact on culture has been far greater. The long format with three-hour conversations has been the perfect platform for scientists, athletes, entrepreneurs, actors, comedians and philosophers to share their ideas with the world. It has democratized information. Millions of people including bus drivers, students, teachers, lawyers, warehouse packers and gardeners have access to some of the best ideas available to mankind. No longer do universities have a monopoly over ideas. The encroaching suppression on free speech with safe spaces on campuses around the world is obliterated by civil discussion. Disagreement is welcomed as Rogan challenges viewpoints he does not agree with. There is debate.

The political landscape is still divisive. There is still clickbait, sound bites, talking points, teleprompters and echo-chambers. But no one could have predicted the Joe Rogan podcast becoming one of the greatest champions of democracy in the Western world. It is a public library of ideas, an arena of discourse.

These claims might seem like a stretch. You may already be skeptical of a book by an unknown author with 'Joe Rogan' in the subtitle. Surely the book will be filled with unfounded conspiracy theories written by a random person on the internet? I hope to prove you wrong – although Alex Jones did nearly make it into the book. For those of you who have never heard of Joe Rogan no background knowledge is required. However you will miss out on the occasional flat earth joke here and there.

There are over 5,000 hours of Joe Rogan's discussions with hundreds of thought-provoking guests. I've heard it said that to become an expert you must do something for 10,000 hours. I suppose this means I am halfway to becoming an expert on The Joe Rogan Experience. I almost have a PHD in BroScience. I listened to the podcast before I could drive a car or knew that DMT was not a smoothie. My background is in writing but I also have a Bachelor of Science from the University of Sydney. This basic level of understanding has allowed me to do further research on many of the science-related guests.

I set myself the mammoth task of sifting through 1,500 episodes to find the most powerful ideas. The only rule is that there is one idea per guest. These ideas come from guests ranging from great scientific thinkers such as Sean Carroll and Neil deGrasse Tyson to U.S. Navy SEAL and endurance athlete David Goggins. However, this book is definitely skewed towards scientists and philosophers. Simply because they tend to devote their lives to the exploration of powerful ideas. This is not to say comedians and others are not as valuable. When writing this book became particularly mentally challenging, I would always switch off the scientists and turn on the comedians. The great comics on the podcast like Joey Diaz, Theo Von and Bill Burr provided laughter, something equally important, especially now. But they were not the focus of this book, and for the same reasons, none of Joe's many celebrity guests made the list – but they do make for great entertainment. They include Robert Downey Jr, Ed Norton, Dan Bilzerian, Mike Tyson, Wiz Khalifa, Tony Hawke and David Lee Roth to name just a few.

For those fellow long-time listeners of JRE this book goes well beyond the podcast. It amalgamates the podcast with information from the guest's independent work such as books, lectures and debates as well as my own research and ideas. I have cited all sources extensively to give credit to the untold number of authors who have informed my exploration of these subjects. However, make no mistake, this book is an original piece of work. The countless analogies, narratives and supplementary studies have taken me a long time to assemble and create.

That's why this book is not just a memory bank or summary of the ideas you have listened to before, it is an expedition into fields of philosophy, psychology, politics and postmodernism. I have endeavored to read each guest's book where they have written one and the process of choosing what to select for each chapter is like trying to pick the best grape in a vineyard. There is a lot of quality content both in the podcast and in the guest's own work that you will miss. I have focused on one idea per guest because it allows me to explore and explain their way of thinking with enough clarity to change your own way of viewing the world. Each chapter could be viewed as a launch pad into twenty-five different perspectives that I hope are radically different from your own. There are ideas presented in this book that can change your life. And this doesn't necessarily mean you will end up being an elk-eating, DMT enthusiast who loves his flotation tank. Although I can make no promises. If you find yourself at any point swearing at the page labeling me a 'globalist cuckold' then I have done my job. The book has challenged your views.

Without exploring these ideas in this form and giving ownership to the fans, we might lose them forever.

Here are the twenty-five most powerful ideas from The Joe Rogan Experience.

DR CARL HART

01. THE WAR ON DRUGS IS INEFFECTIVE

TOPIC: DRUGS
GUEST: NEUROSCIENTIST
PODCAST: #469, #698
WHERE TO FIND MORE: HIGH PRICE (BOOK)

I like historical fiction. It conveys an underlying truth in an engaging story free from the strict rules of historical accuracy. When I found out George W. Bush, a conservative President of the United States, had admitted to smoking marijuana and was silent on his cocaine use, I got creative. I pictured a young George W. Bush doing lines off the oval office desk while portraits of Abraham Lincoln looked at him despairingly. With all his 'coke strength' he was probably moments away from calling Saddam Hussein to challenge him to a personal fist fight. Although this never happened it might not be too far from the truth. Bush's sister-in-law alleges that a young George W. Bush snorted cocaine at Camp David, the country house for the president who at that time was his father George H.W. Bush.[1] The president's own son was alleged to be doing cocaine while his father waged one of the largest wars on drugs in America's history. The president who just thirty years ago held up a bag of crack cocaine on national television to talk of its destructive influence could probably have just asked his son to borrow a bag of his coke instead. The same son who would then become president in 2001 and continue the war on drugs. A battle that had been waged since the seventies.

This battle was playing out in urban areas and ghettos across America. Despite most people never setting foot in these areas, they had seen it in pop-culture. The world was obsessed with the illicit drug trade. People saw the streets of Baltimore overrun with drug kingpins in *The Wire,* they saw narcotics officers betrayed in *Training Day* and they even got to play gang members in *GTA San Andreas.*

Dr Carl Hart didn't watch movies about the projects, he grew up in one. His family lived in South Florida projects during the crack epidemic, the very drug that George H.W. Bush was waging war against in the seventies.

The tale of how Dr Carl Hart rose out of poverty to become a tenured African American professor at an Ivy League university is one of the most incredible stories I have ever heard. His book *High Price* documents the rise of a man who navigated the treacherous waters of poverty and domestic violence to crack cocaine itself. His story is not a self-help book on how anyone can achieve anything. It is far from that. Instead, Dr Carl Hart is a neuropsychopharmacologist and leading researcher on the impacts of illicit drugs on humans. He will show you that everything you think about drugs is wrong. No drug is off-limits, we are going to examine the effects of meth to Adderall to crack to coke. Most policy makers are too afraid to talk about the relative harm of drugs. They prefer to wage all-out war on every drug that is not made by a pharmaceutical company. We are going to go deeper, a lot deeper.

Has the war on drugs been effective?

We must go back in a time machine to 1971. From here, we can trace the origins of why most people in the West believe what they do about illicit drugs. Richard Nixon was the president of the United States, the guy in the glass jar in Futurama. Nixon was facing a fierce backlash for America's continued involvement in the Vietnam War and his handling of racial tensions in America. His opposition, the left, were leading the antiwar movement and the push for racial equality. The left-wing was also into something else, drugs. It was the counterculture movement led by the political left of the sixties and seventies that saw an exponential rise in marijuana and psychedelic drugs.[2] There was research by mainstream institutions into psychedelic drugs for therapy and even discussion of the decriminalization of weed in certain states. When President Nixon declared war on drugs in 1971, he also declared war on his political opposition. Nixon made marijuana a schedule one drug despite a unanimous report recommending decriminalization. As one of his top aides later commented, "We knew we couldn't make it illegal to be either against the war or black, but by getting the public to associate the hippies with marijuana and blacks with heroin, and then criminalizing both heavily, we could disrupt those communities."[3]

And disrupt they did. The war had begun. Nixon invested billions of dollars into the law enforcement machine. The criminal justice system and prison industry exploded. There were now millions of people employed by the U.S. government to fight the war against drugs. Both democratic and republican governments continued this fight for the next fifty years. It grew into a global industry with an army of government agencies in countries all over the world united against one enemy. The drug trade. It seemed like an enemy worth fighting. Everyone has seen the consequences of illicit drugs – the broken families, star athletes who become addicts and the junkies willing to let their babies die for crack. Although, on closer inspection, I realized the only time I had heard of a junkie letting their baby die was from the movie *Trainspotting*. It's a famous and unforgettable scene where a baby lies dead in its crib as her mother is shooting up with a spoon. My sources for my views on drugs were from movies, TV and the media. To find accurate information on drugs I needed to turn to history, science and Dr Carl Hart.

In the eighties while many celebrities, bankers and the president's son sniffed powder cocaine in mansions around America, crack cocaine was being smoked in the hood. It is a tale of two cities and two different drugs. Crack cocaine was cheap to produce so was used by mainly impoverished black communities while powder cocaine was used in predominately rich white neighborhoods. Unfortunately, people's views on the harm of different drugs were being influenced by anecdotes and media reports. The media portrayed crack cocaine as a drug that was so addictive it could ruin lives with a single hit. College graduates were just one puff away from becoming vagrant-crack dropouts. Most people genuinely believed that crack cocaine was so potent it was partly to blame for the poverty and violence in urban America. This belief led to the 1986 legislation that saw the 100 to 1 disparity in sentencing for crack and powder cocaine. Under this legislation, you would need to be carrying 500 grams of powder cocaine to receive the same sentence as someone carrying just five grams of crack. As Dr Hart points out, five grams of cocaine is around 100-200 doses and 500 grams is 10,000-20,000 doses.[4] Crack cocaine and powder cocaine are qualitatively the same drug. Their chemical structures are virtually identical. It is easy to be skeptical of Dr Hart here because if this claim is true, it means that legislation without scientific merit has racially targeted a minority group. It's a serious allegation. It is factually true; independent sources such as the reputable Oxford Treatment Center corroborate that there is no significant difference between the two drugs. In their words, "The two substances are basically chemically identical except that crack cocaine has the hydrochloride salt removed."[5] Removing the hydrochloride salt allows the cocaine to be smoked so the only difference is the route of administration. Crack is smoked and powder coke is snorted. Drugs that are smoked enter the bloodstream faster and give an instantaneous high. However, as the Oxford Treatment Center also acknowledges, there is no evidence that it is more harmful than powder cocaine.[6] It's like the difference between smoking marijuana and consuming edible marijuana. The route of administration influences the intensity and duration of the high but it is still the same active ingredient with the same effects. There is one key difference, the price. The price of crack cocaine was much lower than powdered cocaine thus it was readily available in impoverished communities. People who had very limited employment prospects, health care and financial support now had access to a cheap drug that offered instant pleasure for painful circumstances. The authorities labeled 'crack cocaine' as the villain while the true enemy, poverty, went unnoticed. Under these anti-crack laws, 91 percent of the people incarcerated were black.[7] The same drug when used by different communities had different punishments. Use powdered cocaine and you can become president, use crack cocaine and you will go to jail.

The cost of misinformation on drug use is enormous. While everyone wants to solve the same problem, without a rational and scientific discussion about drugs, the poorest in society suffer. The war on drugs has resulted in the land of the free having the highest incarcerated population in the world. There are 2.2 million people in public and private prisons in America. A disproportionate number are black men imprisoned for minor drug-related offenses. Has the war on drugs been successful? It has been an abject failure on about every conceivable metric. Most importantly, it has not resulted in a decrease in the supply of drugs or drug use.[8] Let that sink in. A billion-dollar war against drug supply has not been able to reduce it at all. Is the enemy the world is fighting worth the cost of war?

Maybe we don't even know what the enemy really is. It's time to address societies' myths about drugs that fuel this futile war. Dr Carl Hart's most important idea is about drawing our attention to the definition of drug addiction. Most people think anyone who uses heroin or meth is a drug addict – I certainly did – although by definition, drug-related addiction must involve the drug impairing their psychosocial functioning.[9] This means drugs have made a person unable to manage responsibilities such as going to work and being a parent. Shockingly, 80-90 percent of users of crack cocaine, heroin and methamphetamine were not addicted.[10] Users of these drugs were members of society capable of maintaining employment and not being substantially impaired by their drug use. This is about the same number as alcohol, with 85-90 percent of users not gaining an addiction.[11] The majority of drug users are not addicted, even for drugs we typically associate as extreme. This challenges the assumption that the war on drugs was built on. It was always assumed that heroin, methamphetamine and crack cocaine would ravage communities causing people's lives to spiral out of control as soon as they tried the drug. Statistically, that is not true. This is not to say that drugs do not pose a large threat to people's physical and mental health – especially those with underlying psychiatric illnesses – they do. The fewer people doing drugs the safer society would be, just as fewer people driving on roads would make society safer. People are always going to want to go places whether it be by car or by drugs; drug policy needs to be smart about how it manages this undeniable reality.

What happens to someone who takes meth you might ask? Dr Carl Hart conducts experiments at an Ivy League institution where he administers methamphetamine to people and studies its effects. In double-blind controlled experiments, participants were given methamphetamine or a placebo. The participants, who were already meth users, were then carefully monitored for twenty-four hours. The results showed that participants given methamphetamine performed better on cognitive tests and reported an elevated mood. There was also a significant increase in blood pressure and heart rate and the participants had only six hours of sleep compared to the control group who had eight. [12] Anyone who has taken Adderall has probably experienced the exact same effects. It shouldn't come as much of a surprise as Adderall and meth are chemically almost identical. One is the most popular study drug in the world used by college students studying medicine and law while the other is meth. College students aren't running around the streets crazed with superhuman methamphetamine strength. They are in libraries using the drug to study.

It's important to understand the implications of Dr Carl Hart's research. It certainly does not mean that people should start taking meth. I feel some people might champion Dr Carl Hart for the wrong reasons. All drugs can have harmful and addictive properties that can cause serious problems for society. The research is not a justification for self-destructive drug use. But the research means we are wrong about the way we view drugs. It means that media, pop culture and big industry has shaped our societal perceptions about what drugs are bad and what drugs are good without scientific input. Alcohol is fine. Smoking is okay. Meth is terrible. Powder coke is permissible but crack is not. The consequence of these perceptions are misinformed drug policies that demonize certain categories of drugs while others are legal – despite them all having similar detrimental consequences to society. Alcohol and tobacco have repeatedly been shown to have the most negative effects on society out of all drug use.[13] While this is in part because they are the most prevalent, it is hard to make a case that tobacco causes anything but lung cancer. Yet societies are willing to allow adults to make their own choices about whether they want a tequila shot or a drag of a cigarette. For many people around the world who choose to use illicit drugs such as marijuana, the greatest threat is not the drug but the law itself. Being incarcerated and having future employment prospects restricted for recreational drug use is a far greater consequence than any known effects of taking the drug.

So what do we do about it?

Drug decriminalization might be the answer according to Dr Hart. Portugal provides evidence that such a policy can be effective. In 2001, the country decriminalized all illegal drugs.[14] People who were caught with any drug were issued with an infringement notice and had to appear in front of a panel consisting of social workers and psychologists – and no police. The panel tries to address the underlying issues of the drug user. Repeat offenders are not imprisoned but instead lose the right to drive and visit certain areas known for drug sales. The country has experienced a reduction in drug-related deaths and drug use more broadly. Although the reductions are only moderate, it is far more effective than a policy that uses law enforcement to imprison a significant proportion of the population. Drug users are not excluded from the economy and society.

I remember walking through the streets of Tokyo at around 11am in the morning with some friends. A Japanese businessman wearing a suit burst out of the doors of a nightclub. He was to this day the drunkest man I have ever seen. The man could barely walk and was so drunk that he thought we spoke Japanese despite being the whitest people in Tokyo. We all thought it was hilarious. Looking back at it that man probably had a pretty troubled relationship with alcohol. It was 11am on a Tuesday. His alcohol use could have been destroying his family life at home. But what's certain is that he could stroll past law enforcement, stumble into a cab and get home. He wasn't going to go to jail for drinking, no matter how bad his alcoholism was. Alcohol might destroy his life but imprisonment would not. He would have a fighting chance of restoring his life without a criminal record. The enemy is not drugs, the enemy is the biological and social causes that lead people to abuse them.

It is time for the war on drugs to come to an end.

NEIL DEGRASSE TYSON

02. THE COSMIC PERSPECTIVE IS ESSENTIAL

TOPIC: SPACE
GUEST: ASTROPHYSICIST
PODCAST: #310, #919, #1159, #1347
WHERE TO FIND MORE:
ASTROPHYSICS FOR PEOPLE IN A HURRY (BOOK)

Why did humans want to go to the Moon?
Why do humans want to go into space?
Why do humans want to colonize Mars?

These questions have been asked many times over the past century. To many people it seems an injustice that billions of dollars are spent on national space programs while people starve. NASA's budget alone is US$22.6 billion with the U.S. government spending a total of US$650 billion since the space agency's inception. How can such frivolous spending be justified on something that doesn't directly advance the welfare of people in need?

President John F. Kennedy grappled with this question. In 1962 in his speech at Rice University he outlined his reasoning to the American people, including the now-famous phrase:

"We choose to go to the Moon not because it is easy but because it is hard."[15]

On July 20, 1969, Neil Armstrong became the first human to step on the Moon. All around the world people watched on primitive televisions as history unfolded before their eyes. Humans had done the impossible. It took billions of dollars and thousands of minds to achieve such a feat. Was it worth it? With that amount of resources global problems such as poverty, HIV and world hunger surely could have been solved. President Kennedy's call to go the Moon for the ultimate human challenge seems to be less convincing than the call to address all human suffering in the world.

There is a better speech about the Moon from another sitting president which most people have not heard. There is a good reason the public is not familiar with the speech – it was written for President Richard Nixon to cover the possibility that Neil Armstrong and Buzz Aldrin died during the Moon landing. If they had, how would the president justify the enormous financial expenditure and the death of the astronauts on live television? Nixon would have said this:

FOR EVERY HUMAN BEING WHO LOOKS UP AT THE MOON IN THE NIGHTS TO COME WILL KNOW THAT THERE IS SOME CORNER OF ANOTHER WORLD THAT IS FOREVER MANKIND.[16]

This is far more captivating in my opinion. Humans went to the Moon not just because it was the ultimate challenge but because it forever altered our place in the cosmos. It showed us how small our planet really is. And the ramifications of that are profound – so much so they justified billions and billions of dollars and even the lives of the courageous astronauts who have died in space. The Moon landing provided humanity with a greater appreciation for both its achievement and insignificance. It provided the world with a cosmic perspective.

Neil deGrasse Tyson argues this is why humans should care about space. A cosmic perspective. It provides us with an invaluable outlook, one in which we gain a greater sense of meaning as we understand our place in the four-dimensional fabric of space-time. To communicate this idea requires us to navigate through the galaxy encountering supernovas and black holes. Thankfully, our next guest is equipped to take us to all of these places. Neil deGrasse Tyson (NDT) is one of the world's most famous astrophysicists and science communicators. He has frequented the podcast and episode #919 is a notable appearance as he arrives wearing a suit and wide-brimmed cowboy hat. He can't decide between getting the call up to explore the Martian frontiers or looking professional for the podcast. Not that Joe would give a shit. Either way, he is always ready to talk about the universe and is the only guest where Rogan has spoken for about a minute of the three-hour podcast. He really does love to talk about space.

Once upon a time, roughly 13.8 billion years ago, our entire universe was condensed into a point that was one-trillionth the size of the period that ends this sentence.[17] This is how NDT opens his book, *Astrophysics for People in a Hurry*. It really is the most elegant way of capturing how every piece of matter in the universe was condensed into a pinpoint so small it practically didn't exist. Then the big bang happened.

The first second of the universe was eventful to say the least. Within a billionth of a billionth of a billionth of a billionth of a second after the big bang, cosmic inflation started. The universe began to expand, rapidly. That basically indivisible pinpoint became the size of a basketball.[18] Then when the universe was a millionth of a millionth of a second old a phenomenon called the Higgs field began to cool the unfathomably hot universe.

After the universe was just one second old, the first elements were born – hydrogen, helium and lithium. There was still a long, long way to go before the universe would give birth to conscious creatures capable of tracing the origins of the galaxy – creatures that could talk about DMT, monkeys and elk for hours.

For the next billion years the universe kept expanding as its temperature dropped. Early matter was uniformly distributed throughout space but denser regions began to pull other matter together as they concentrated into galaxies.[19] This process looked like steam filling a room, then slowly coming together to form an ice sculpture. Dense regions in space formed gaseous clouds of hydrogen and helium. These clouds gave birth to stars. These stars gave birth to us.

The cores of these early stars were so hot that they gave rise to nuclear reactions, causing heavier elements to form. Scientists get particularly poetic when talking about our relationship to stars. In the words of NDT, these high mass stars, "fortuitously explode, scattering their chemically enriched guts throughout the universe."[20] It is from these exploded guts that heavier elements such as carbon, nitrogen and oxygen are found. All of which are required for making life as we know it.

In the words of Lawrence Krauss, another dreamy-eyed astrophysicist:

> "every atom in your body was once inside a star that exploded. Our bodies are made of stardust."[21]

Fast-forward to the present and we now live in a universe with more than 170 billion galaxies. The most common type of galaxy is a spiral galaxy which holds around 100 billion stars. These spiral galaxies look like a twisted hand with each finger a different branch of billions of stars. Some simple arithmetic reveals there are more stars in the universe than there are grains of sand on Earth.[22]

Our galaxy, the Milky Way, is a spiral galaxy. It is of little significance from a cosmic point of view and, out of its billions of stars, there is a relatively insignificant one called the Sun. This isn't sarcasm, the Sun really isn't that special, it's about the size of an average star with fairly normal properties. Some stars – such as UY Scuti – have a radius 1,700 times larger. Just like New York City, the Sun is one of the most overhyped things in the universe.

The Sun was formed nine billion years ago from a gaseous cloud of heavier elements. This spawned rocky debris that began to orbit around this enormous fiery ball of mass, giving rise to what we call our solar system. Within our solar system there are eight planets including our pale blue dot. Earth. The only known planet to house sentient life. But not sentient enough to find other life that surely abounds in the universe. Aliens and Joe Rogan are a topic for another book.

One thing that NDT emphasizes when speaking about Earth are the 'Goldilocks Conditions' for life. The odds of our oceans being in liquid form is something we take for granted, but had we been a bit closer to the Sun they would have evaporated and had we been a bit farther away they would be frozen. Our orbit miraculously allowed these chemically rich liquid oceans from which life was born.[23]

Jupiter is known for many things but protecting the Earth is not usually one of them. Our planet is on a peaceful orbit in the inner solar system while Jupiter must contend with hostile asteroids flying in its direction from the nearby asteroid belt.[24] The huge planet has a gravitational field that is many times stronger than here on Earth and acts as a shield, protecting us from asteroids that would otherwise be hurtling in our direction. Humans got pretty lucky.

But that luck doesn't last forever. As we conduct our day to day lives with concerns ranging from missing a deadline to forgetting a friend's birthday, a much bigger threat looms over our heads. A meteorite that slips through the cracks.

This happened 65 million years ago, when an asteroid the size of Mount Everest collided with Earth, smashing into the Yutcan Peninsula off the coast of Mexico. It was around this time that virtually all dinosaurs went extinct. The most dominant species on the planet did not stand a chance against the cosmic collision that rocked the entire planet.

Earth exists in a pretty hostile universe. As well as meteorites and comets, there are also black holes to deal with. These are holes in the fabric of space-time that are so powerful that not even light can escape; everything within their reach is consumed. There is a black hole at the center of our galaxy called Sagittarius A which has been inhaling planets, stars and light for some time now.

So what's the point of all this information about space? Is Neil deGrasse Tyson just a Bill Nye the Science Guy for adults? What value is there in learning about space online with NDT and a comedian who loves to talk about black holes and the space-time continuum?

The cosmic perspective we gain from learning about space offers humanity something very powerful, almost spiritual. It gives us a philosophy. Throughout our short stint on Earth, all humans have looked up at the same Moon, all with different sets of worries and dreams. And even when these dreams are realized, the worries faded and the humans dead, the Moon will live on. The Sun will keep going and the Earth will keep spinning. After the last human has walked the Earth, the Sun will still be there. And one day when the Sun explodes it will not be bright enough for faraway planets to see. The Sun is too small to make a supernova explosion and our solar system will be effaced from space without even a blink in the night skies of planets around the galaxy. Our history will be forgotten and every trace of our existence gone.

In a trillion years, space will have expanded so far that no galaxies will be observable from our own.[25] Anyone looking for them would conclude that space is just a dark void of nothingness with no other stars, supernovas or galaxies. The universe as we know it today will be lost.

Space does not only teach us of our impermanence but also of our ignorance. We don't know what dark matter is, the mysterious invisible dark energy that makes up most of the universe's mass, holding galaxies together. Scientists are certain of its existence but clueless about what it is. The predominant force in the universe is unknown.

The most valuable idea from Neil deGrasse Tyson is not learning random facts about space but the cosmic perspective we gain. If you will allow me to get very philosophical, speculative, unscientific and pretentious, the universe teaches us to dissolve our egos. Inevitably, every history book, statue and monument built in a human's name will disappear forever. Our pale blue dot will be recycled by the universe, every atom repurposed for something else. The universe will exist for eternity and the stardust we were born from will return to stardust. The only comfort we can take is that we are a part of a great cosmic chain that is infinitely greater than ourselves.

Take a moment to appreciate this cosmic chain that we all belong to. NDT does some basic calculations to show that some of the water you have drunk has passed through people like Genghis Khan, Socrates and Joan of Arc.[26] Even the air you breathe has been previously given life to Beethoven, Gandhi and Isaac Newton. Everything is interconnected from our shared origin as a single cell organism to the common birth of every element in the universe, the Big Bang. To accept our place in this cosmic chain of existence is liberating.

"We simply do not live in this universe. This universe lies within us."[27] NDT

EDWARD SNOWDEN

03. DIGITAL PRIVACY IS A RIGHT

TOPIC: MASS SURVEILLANCE
GUEST: WHISTLEBLOWER
PODCAST: #1368
WHERE TO FIND MORE:
PERMANENT RECORD (BOOK)

What is the worst thing you have ever done? Hidden in your subconscious are memories of mistakes that will not go away. Mistakes that could compromise every aspect of your life – your job, your citizenship and even your relationship with your family. These mistakes could range from one inappropriate comment made decades ago, or previous illicit drug use to just talking to the wrong person. Everyone has made mistakes and kept secrets from people they love.

There are people whose job it is to exploit these mistakes for their benefit. Once they find compromising pieces of information, they can manipulate us; secrets are a valuable commodity. Everyone is vulnerable to this exploitation no matter how unimportant a life they think they lead.

The industry that deals in secrets is the intelligence community. All around the world, countries have intelligence agencies using their power covertly to manipulate the course of the future. Little is known about the highly secretive world of spies. The next guest on the podcast used to work in this mysterious branch of government for both the CIA and NSA. His name is Edward Snowden. He appears on the podcast via Skype and is not present in the studio as he streams from Moscow, Russia. He is a political exile and fugitive, with every arm of the U.S. government attempting to extradite him and put him in prison. Why is this politely spoken young man on the run?

Edward Snowden has sacrificed his life for the next idea. This idea is that democracies must protect the right to digital privacy.

Here is how your freedom has been taken away without you realizing.

The American intelligence community has a long history and has been involved in collecting intelligence since 1947. All around the world, comparable agencies exist such as the Australian Secret Intelligence Service, Russia's Foreign Intelligence Service and the United Kingdom's famous MI6. This global network of spies forms an underbelly of government that most citizens never get to glimpse. When people imagine spies, images of James Bond come rushing to mind as he consumes martinis with beautiful women as some egotistical villain with a niche weapon of destruction tries to take over the world. While only a movie, there is some truth to this bygone era of espionage. Snowden recounts witnessing these old school agents in the field. The CIA deploys agents called COs (Case Officers) to collect human intelligence. In Snowden's own words they are, "terminal cynics, charming liars who smoked and drank."[28]

While deployed in Geneva, Switzerland, to gather digital intelligence, Snowden was invited to a party with a CO. The CIA's presence in Geneva was strategic. It was a hotbed of bureaucrats from the UN, rich Saudi Arabian oil sheiks and other elusive figures drawn in by Switzerland's secretive financial system. All of these types of people attended embassy parties – where Snowden now joined them.

The CO identified a potential target, a Saudi involved in financial management. The field agent wanted to develop a 'relationship' for information. He spent months trying to form a friendship but this strategy was not working so he resorted to another. One night he got the Saudi financier incredibly drunk and then encouraged him to drive home. The Saudi got into his car far too drunk to drive. The CIA agent then called the Swiss police and gave them the Saudi's license plate. After being arrested, his license was suspended and he was given a huge fine.[29] None other than the CIA agent himself offered to bail him out and drive him to work each day as a display of 'friendship.' He would never have known it was the agent who got him in this mess in the first place.

Eventually, the CIA agent asked for information and the Saudi realized he did not have genuine intentions, he stopped talking to the agent and now had a drink driving offense on his record.

This is old school spycraft. Good old face-to-face manipulation using money, power and tricks to maneuver people into giving information. Governments are willing to exploit individuals for their own gain, whether it be abetting illegal activity, giving them a criminal record or blackmailing them – using their secrets as leverage. Society is not outraged by these methods when used against enemies but what happens when these methods are used on their citizens?

Welcome to the new school of spies. They are not charismatic drinkers like James Bond; they are introverted computer people like Edward Snowden. Governments realized that collecting human intelligence was becoming obsolete when all the information they need lies in the pockets of most humans who walk the Earth. Smartphones. These devices record every movement we make, constantly logging our activity to a cellular tower. Each phone has a unique identifier that the cellular tower then logs into its database. Phone providers know exactly who we speak to, how long we speak for, and where we are. Apps on these phones know even more about us; they know what we search, who we message and what we buy. This is called metadata. Hidden in this data are our deepest darkest secrets – all stored digitally and able to be kept permanently by companies. The intelligence community realized this was the most powerful tool they could use.

There was a time not so long ago when you could roam through a city, talk to a stranger and buy a pack of cigarettes completely unnoticed. It was an abstract concept to pinpoint exactly where you were as there were no surveillance cameras, GPS phone trackers or Apple Pay. Companies could not pay to know where you were and governments could not track you down without having people on the ground. This was a freedom that humans in even history's most oppressive regimes possessed. If people could not see them, they could not be monitored. After 9/11, this was about to change.

The NSA, America's National Security Agency, was humiliated after a failure of intelligence resulted in the largest terror attack the country had ever seen. Their historical brief of 'targeted collection of communication' was switched to 'bulk collection.' This is another way of saying mass surveillance. The threat of terror was used by agencies to expand their power and influence to bypass the constitution. This was happening around the democratic world as governments such as the U.K. invested heavily in their intelligence capabilities. A nefarious 'deep state' was created. The deep state is not a conspiracy, it is the unfortunate reality that governments are now made up of tens of thousands of unelected intelligence officers, military officers and law enforcement who decide highly secretive policy without consent from the public. A report written by those within the deep state acknowledged that members were usually loyal to their agency over the government.[30] This means the legions of people influencing policy are serving their agencies' agendas over the people they were sworn to serve. The deep state was undermining democracy.

Edward Snowden worked in the depths of this shadow state for both the NSA and CIA as a systems administrator. Basically, he was in charge of ensuring the networks for these organizations remained operational. Being a systems admin gave him unparalleled access to everything that was on the network. Here, he first found the NSA's program called PRISM; an unprecedented program of mass surveillance on a civilian population.

Before the 2013 leaks, only a dozen or so people knew the true extent of the mass surveillance program that was going on in the United States. Snowden was one of these people. PRISM was a mass data collection program where information on all citizens was stored without a warrant. The NSA was receiving all the call logs of customers of companies such as Verizon, along with other personal data from Google and Amazon. They stored this private information in massive data centers in highly secretive facilities such as the Utah Data Center. The government was illegally gathering information about you and everyone you know to be used if the need arose. Other democratic countries had similar programs. It was as if they were creating secret museums of our lives and allowing tour groups to view every aspect of our existence without our permission.

It gets worse, much worse. The NSA also had a program called XKEYSCORE[31] which enabled agents to search nearly everything a user does on the internet. All that was required was a telephone number or IP address for their entire activity log online to become available. An NSA agent could pry into your life without having any suspicion of you committing a crime – they could simply type your details into a machine and find your deepest darkest secrets. No one was immune to the curiosity of those who had access to the most intrusive government program created;

celebrities, politicians and even lovers were all fair game. In Snowden's book *Permanent Record*, he revealed a practice known as LOVEINT. Love intelligence is fairly self-explanatory; it involved agents using the program to monitor their lovers' activity, including listening to phone calls and watching their activity online.

The scope of the program is horrifying. Agents could hijack webcams, listen to microphones and violate every modicum of privacy with little oversight. Snowden reports watching the webcam of an Iranian professor as he sat with his son searching on his desktop computer. The man was guilty of no crime, but the agents sat and listened to his child's laughter from the other side of the world.[32] Such a pure human interaction was now subject to intrusion from unelected and unsupported government programs. Maybe the people who covered their webcams weren't so crazy after all?

Our right to digital privacy is being violated but many will say it shouldn't matter if you have nothing to hide. Why would a law-abiding citizen who occasionally indulges in watching softcore porn care if they were being watched? Their existence is mundane, from the type of work they do to the type of porn they watch. They live in a neighborhood where everything is safe and the worst thing they have done is jaywalk across an empty street. Why should privacy matter to these squeaky clean vanilla citizens?

The right to digital privacy is the only thing that prevents the government from having totalitarian power over people. This is such a great threat that 50 percent of America's Bill of Rights is made up of ten amendments intended to make the job of law enforcement harder.[33] This is true in any democratic nation. Government is given limited power by the people for the people. It is not the government who give limited power to the people for the government. Any law enforcement that wields so much power is a direct threat to the freedom of citizens. Imagine law enforcement who don't have to ask for a warrant – they can simply peruse your decades-long digital footprint. They can find instances of you committing minor infringements – jaywalking perhaps – and suddenly they hold power over the course of your entire life. Perhaps you become a politician and intelligence agencies leverage information they have obtained unlawfully from your past to influence you in government. Photos of you doing cocaine in college or messages you sent to a past lover. To cede your control over your digital privacy is to cede your freedom as a democratic citizen, no matter how mundane your digital history might be.

At what point do these programs designed to 'protect us' become the very thing we are trying to protect ourselves against. China is a totalitarian state whose citizens enjoy almost no personal freedom, with no access to the public internet and restrictions on who can travel internationally. Their government openly uses methods of mass surveillance to ensure control of its citizens. Many have now heard of the infamous social credit system. This system involves the Chinese government collecting data on all citizens and giving them a score based on their obedience to the state. Using millions of security cameras, AI algorithms and digital data, they are attempting to rank their 1.4 billion citizens. Things such as jaywalking will result in a drop in your social credit score.[34] Messaging people with low social credit scores will lower your own. People with low social credit scores will not be able to take loans, travel or send their kids to good schools. If this sounds like some form of dystopian hell, that's because it is.

The only thing that differentiates democratic nations is that individuals are free to do whatever they want provided they don't break the law. But how can any of us be free if the government is recording every step we take, every message we make and every item we purchase? Freedom simply does not exist if our data is not private. Allowing intelligence agencies to have this power is to be one step closer to an authoritarian regime like China.

Edward Snowden is a wanted man. The U.S. government wants to place him in prison because he exposed a deep state that prefers to hide in the shadows. He showed people that the government was not protecting their freedoms; it was taking them away. The Joe Rogan platform allowed a fugitive to deliver a very powerful message.

Reclaim your digital privacy or forever lose your freedom.

The government is watching.

MATTHEW WALKER

04. SLEEP IS A SUPERPOWER

TOPIC: DREAMS & SLEEP
GUEST: NEUROSCIENTIST
PODCAST: #1109
WHERE TO FIND MORE: WHY WE SLEEP (BOOK)

Thomas Edison had many light bulb moments. He did invent the light bulb after all. He also invented film, the movie camera, automatic telegraphs, the alkaline storage battery and held a total of 1,093 U.S. patents for his other inventions.

Edison also loved to take naps. The great inventor would relax into his comfortable chair and fall asleep at his desk. Although his naps were more eccentric then it might appear. In both of his hands, he would hold a metal ball bearing. Once he had fallen into a deep slumber and every muscle in his body had relaxed, the ball bearings would become dislodged from his hands and fall onto the floorboards abruptly waking Edison from his sleep. It was like a human alarm clock that would have almost certainly pissed off everyone in the house. Without delay, Edison would then write on his notepad whatever thoughts had come to him while he slept. Many of these post-nap thoughts changed the world forever.[35] It was as if Edison was charting the unknown realms of his subconscious sleeping brain in search of ideas. Like a Spanish explorer who borrowed ideas from another civilization only to return home and present them as his. Maybe my imagination is getting carried away. After all, sleep shouldn't be interesting; it is the very thing we do when something is boring.

Sleep, however, may be one of the last remaining human mysteries. We spend almost a third of our lives in this state of poorly understood consciousness. Each night billions of people close their eyes as they enter the hallucinatory state of the dream world. And each morning billions of people awaken with only the faintest memory of the delusions, fantasies and visions they just experienced. During a typical lifetime, people spend an average of six years dreaming.[36] This got me thinking. Six years equals 52,560 hours which equals 3,153,600 minutes. The average running time for a movie is roughly 100 minutes. So you have watched 31,536 feature-length films worth of dreams. When you think of the impact your ten favorite movies have had on your life, it is almost impossible to quantify the potential impact that dreams subconsciously exert on us. Behind each memorable day in our life is a night's forgotten dream – and we have no idea how it influenced our actions. Sleep and dreams might be the final frontier for exploration. So why do we sleep?

I first listened to the podcast with Matthew Walker late at night. My laptop shone brightly in my eyes as midnight approached. Walker is a neuroscience professor at the University of California, Los Angeles who specializes in sleep research. He left me with a bit of a dilemma. He was so captivating that I wanted to stay up all night and listen to him yet everything he was saying was demanding I fall asleep. I chose to listen about sleep instead of actually sleeping. After listening to the entire podcast I regretted my decision – then after reading his book *Why We Sleep,* I really regretted my decision. Walker provides the most comprehensive scientific argument for why sleep is a human superpower and how we can harness it. Sleep can make or ruin your life...

But why do we dream? For me, this question must be answered before finding out why we sleep. There are two basic types of sleep. Rapid eye movement (REM) sleep and non-REM sleep. REM-sleep is where we experience our most vivid dreams. It is a unique state of consciousness where, as seen by MRI scans, the body is effectively paralyzed while the brain is incredibly active. There is significant activity in visuospatial regions, the motor cortex, the hippocampus and the limbic system.[37] These regions of the brain are mostly associated with vision, movement, emotion and our autobiographical memory. Most importantly, there is significant deactivation in the prefrontal cortex. This part of the brain is in charge of planning, decision making and regulating social behavior. It's basically the responsible parent of our minds. I have created a simple analogy to understand the science Professor Walker is talking about. REM-sleep is like parents leaving their children in a free house for the weekend, locking all the doors and taking away the key. The kids will go wild as there are no rules to abide by. But thankfully, the doors are locked so they can't leave the house and do any damage. Similarly, in REM-sleep, the body is paralyzed; you can't act out your dreams. Because the parent of our minds (the prefrontal cortex) does not inhibit dreams, they involve highly emotional, vivid and largely nonsensical displays of madness. However, there is always a method to the madness as REM-sleep dreaming plays a vital function in our mental health. Professor Walker's research focuses on how dreams serve as emotional therapy. Are dreams your nighttime psychologist?

The theory is that REM-sleep dreaming reduces the pain of traumatic, emotional episodes during the day by offering emotional resolutions the next morning.[38] The theory seems farfetched, suggesting dreaming is like the reset button on our emotional speedometers. What evidence does Walker have to make such a claim? The theory was based on the remarkable fact that REM-sleep is the only time in your life when there is no noradrenaline in your brain. This is a chemical that is essential to your stress response, an anxiety-triggering molecule.[39] For the 31,536 feature-length films worth of dreams we watch in our lives, our minds essentially can't get stressed. It's as if we could watch *The Shining*, *The Exorcist* and *The Conjuring* without the slightest worry in the world. Professor Walker doesn't talk about movies but instead our emotional memories. He posits that this low-stress mental environment provides the perfect opportunity for our brains to unpack traumatic and emotional memories. This processing reduces the associated pain of the memory. Our dreams allow us to confront things that our conscious brains might be too afraid to. The question remains – what evidence is there for this theory other than the brain's chemical state?

Walker made a prediction. If REM-sleep acted as a form of overnight therapy, it would be expected that an increase in REM-sleep should result in a decrease in the emotional response to an emotive memory. Participants in the experiment were shown emotionally charged images and put into brain scanning machines. Half of the participants were shown the images again after they had a full night's sleep and the other half were shown the images again before they slept. The first group had their sleep monitored for how much REM-sleep they had. This showed the amount of time they were in the vivid dream state. Incredibly, those who had high levels of REM-sleep dreaming had far less emotional activation when viewing the images for a second time the next morning. The second group, who had not been able to sleep/dream between viewing the images, were visibly more distressed on seeing them for a second time. Their amygdala, the area of the brain associated with fear and aggression responses, would light up on brain scans.[40] So why pay for an expensive shrink who somehow owns an Aston Martin when you could just consult your bed for free? It's a remarkable discovery that confirmed Walker's initial theory. Dreams heal. More evidence has confirmed that dreaming acts as an overnight therapist. It tempers the sting of emotional memories and can allow us to explore our darkest moments without anxiety. Welcome to the dream world.

Edison must have been onto something. Research has confirmed that creativity and problem-solving ability is directly enhanced after someone wakes from sleep.[41] Edison benefited from this fact by complete accident. In fact, he despised sleep – it was an enemy of productivity in his eyes. So much so he denounced people who sleep too much as lazy and stated, "there is really no reason to go to bed at all." Sadly, Edison has left the most destructive legacy for human sleep in all of human history. We will soon find out why.

Everyone has encountered a person who claims they need barely any sleep to function perfectly. These are the type of people who drink black coffee, have cold showers and listen to David Goggins. A myth has been perpetuated in our capitalist society that the more we work and the less we sleep, the better off we will be. The myth is so entrenched in our culture that phrases such as 'I will sleep when I am dead' are deemed aspirational in many self-help communities. The sleep-deprived are heroes and those who slept too much are sloths, lazy and unmotivated.

This narrative of sleep is wrong. Dangerously wrong. Take for instance those people who claim they only need five hours of sleep a night. Walker presents laboratory experiments where healthy young males in their mid-twenties are allowed five hours of sleep a night for just one week. Then sample their hormone levels and there will be a statistically significant drop in testosterone compared to their baseline at the beginning of the week. The drop is so substantial that it has effectively aged the participants by 10-15 years in terms of testosterone virility.[42] Your testicles are smaller if you don't sleep says Professor Walker – who must have some pretty big balls to say so to the likes of Jocko Willink. Jocko has so much testosterone he probably needs to sacrifice some to avoid morphing into a gorilla.

What is the cost of people not getting enough sleep? In developed countries, two-thirds of the population do not meet the recommended eight hours of nightly sleep.[43] And the quality of the sleep we are having is greatly reduced by the rampant use of sleeping pills, electronic screens, caffeine, alcohol and regularized temperatures. Let's look at the evidence for why our sleeping habits are quite literally killing us. Every year you unknowingly take part in the largest sleep experiment in the world – daylight savings. In spring we lose just one hour of sleep as we wind our clocks forward. If you examine hospital records for this day (as scientists such as Walker do) there is a 24 percent subsequent increase in heart attacks. Incredibly, in the fall when we gain one hour of sleep, there is a significant reduction in heart attacks on this one day alone.[44] Sleep can save lives.

Why else do we sleep other than trying to avoid heart attacks? The lack of proper sleep has been shown to suppress our immune system, increase risk of cancer, increase the prevalence of mental illness and has even been linked to dementia.[45] Walker has devoted most of his life to exposing the consequences of inadequate sleep. They are clear. There is not a single major organ in the body or process within the brain that isn't optimally enhanced by sleep. If your primary goal in life is being an athlete, sleep might be the performance-enhancing drug you were looking for. Study participants who received less than six hours of sleep a night experienced a 10-30 percent reduction in time taken to reach physical exhaustion. They also experienced a reduction in vertical jump height, decreased muscle strength and faster lactic acid build-up.[46] Simply put, the athlete who trains for longer but sleeps less might as well not be training.

If your primary goal in life requires cognition, the results are equally frightening. Professor Walker's laboratory subjects showed a 40 percent reduction in memory merely by changing the amount of sleep they had for a night. It's hard to translate what a 40 percent reduction of memory looks like in the real world.[47] It could be the difference between people who remember the name of everyone they meet and the assholes who call everyone buddy. It could be the difference between failing a history exam versus being top of the class. Sleep provides an advantage which most health products could only dream they had. Sleep is not only a performance-enhancing drug. It is a superpower.

It's no secret the modern world has ruined our sleep. Thanks to Edison, there are now millions of light bulbs, all of which disrupt our natural circadian rhythm; the body's biological alarm clock. Our natural alarm clock uses light and temperature to signal the release of hormones such as melatonin responsible for making us feel ready to go to bed. Man harnessing light has led to a never-ending display of screens, neon lights and lamps as we no longer fall asleep with the night sky. Walker provides scientifically proven strategies to improve your sleep quality. And they can change your life. It might seem paradoxical but these revolutionary sleeping strategies are just natural habits we lost during the industrial age. They are the opposite of revolutionary. They are natural.

Walker's book provides an excellent synopsis of all the strategies.[18] Here is a list of science-based tips to improve the quality of your sleep.

- Stick to a sleep schedule. Go to bed and wake up at the same time each day.
- Exercise every day but not before you go to bed (one to two hours before).
- Avoid caffeine and nicotine.
- Avoid large meals or beverages late at night.
- Take a hot bath before bed.
- Keep the temperature in your bedroom cool.
- Get sunlight exposure in the day.

There are too many to go into detail here so instead, I will focus on the most important. The first is to ensure you go to sleep and wake up at the same time every day, even on weekends. This will allow your circadian rhythm to kick in and you will naturally generate the melatonin that signals your body when to fall asleep. The next strategy has to do with temperature control. Being cold at night signals to your brain that it is time to fall asleep. The ideal temperature for your room is 65 °F (18.3°C). Our bodies have evolved over millions of years to recognize a drop in temperature as a signal that it is time to go to bed as the sun fades away. Finally, don't use screens before you go to bed. The blue light in your phone or laptop tricks your brain into thinking it is still daytime even though it's midnight. Even when you are watching a sleep scientist telling you exactly how you are being tricked, you are still tricked.

Sleeping in just might be the most productive thing we do all day.

CHRISTOPHER RYAN

05. MARRIAGE WAS NOT MADE FOR HUMANS

TOPIC: SEX
GUEST: PSYCHOLOGIST
PODCAST: #306, #421, #468, #614 +
WHERE TO FIND MORE: SEX AT DAWN (BOOK)

In central North America lives a rodent called the prairie vole. This rodent was affectionately called the 'Christian vole' for some time as it is among the tiny percentage (3-5 percent) of mammals that form a lifelong bond with a partner. It is easy to see why Christians were quick to adopt the faithful rodent as one of their own. The prairie vole seemed to remind humans that if a rodent could be married to one animal at a time, then we too should have no difficulty practicing monogamy. Unfortunately for Pastors around the world, prairie voles are degenerates. It was soon discovered that the Christian vole – while socially monogamous actually lived a life of sexual promiscuity. The prairie voles were closer to Tiger Woods' lifestyle than they were to Jesus.

Ask anyone you know and they will probably tell you that marriage or pair-bonding is the natural way humans mate. Dating television shows are a billion-dollar industry with every type of twist you can imagine. There has been *Date my Mum, Dating in the Dark, The Bachelor, Love Island, Dating Naked and Farmer Wants a Wife* (my favorite Australian one). Despite the bizarre formats of these shows, they all have one thing in common. Love is between two people. The idea is so entrenched in our culture that it is not up for debate. The idea that pair-bonding is the natural condition of humans is labeled as fact in our religious, cultural and even scientific texts. From rom-coms to the Bible, it is clear that a man and a woman were made for each other like ketchup and fries. But is this actually true? (French people have mayonnaise with fries and are also renowned adulterers so maybe they already know the answer).

Marriage is not the natural mating state for humans according to Christopher Ryan. If he is correct, it has major ramifications for Western civilization. It means the institution of marriage is up against hundreds of thousands of years of human evolution. Our relationships are doomed. This controversial argument is made in full in his NYT best-selling book *Sex at Dawn*. The book is so controversial that it spawned another book called *Sex at Dusk* which focuses entirely on criticism of Ryan's initial work. This level of emotive backlash is usually a good sign that you have challenged conventional wisdom. But before we understand this radical proposition, we must examine why some scientists believe that pair-bonding or marriage has been the natural state of human mating. This is called the standard narrative of human sexuality. It's time for a sex education.

The standard narrative is that men and women are in a conflict of genetic agendas. The male sexual agenda is to spread their genes by disseminating sperm to as many potential partners as possible (think Genghis Khan). This is because sperm in a biological sense is cheap and plentiful. Conversely, females possess a finite number of eggs and the cost of raising a child is so great they are highly selective of who they mate with. This is the basic conflict. Sex is inherently less costly for males so they are far more likely to pursue it. Evidence for this includes studies where males were approached by random members of the opposite gender who ask for sex. Not surprisingly, 75 percent of males accepted. When men and women changed roles, zero percent of females accepted the offer from the random male in the experiment.[49] It seems fairly intuitive; males are horny and always willing to have sex. It does little to explain how pair-bonding (marriage) arose in the human species. That is where a concept called parental investment is relevant.

Parental investment is defined as any parental expenditure (time, energy, resources) that benefits the offspring. The parental investment theory suggests that the gender that invests more into its offspring will be more selective in its sexual partner. So in humans, as the cost of childbirth is greater for females, they will be more selective of who they mate with. Thus there is more male competition for mating. The opposite can be observed in nature. For example, the pipefish seahorse is an example of a species where the male will invest more in its offspring. As a result, female pipefish seahorses compete for a male partner. In species such as this, the females will generally be more aggressive, brightly colored and larger than males. Bret Weinstein is an evolutionary biologist who discusses this in more depth on Rogan's podcast. He links this to a provocative scientific argument for why men find some women beautiful but not hot and some hot but not beautiful.[50] I'll reference the clip for those journalists looking for some nice outrage to feed the news cycle.

Let's return to humans where females are generally more selective. They are more selective of male partners as they want a partner who will invest the most resources into the child. This will increase the chance that their offspring will survive – the ultimate goal of Darwin's natural selection. So females want a male partner to form a life-long pair-bond to have increased access to food and shelter, and guarantee the child's protection. They want marriage. The question is why do men stay? After all, we have discussed how promiscuous males are and how cheap sex is to them – so what does conventional evolutionary theory say?

We must go further down the rabbit hole and understand two important biological concepts: concealed ovulation and extended receptivity. Ovulation refers to the release of an egg by a female during her menstrual cycle. It is when she is fertile and capable of conceiving a baby. On average, there are only seven days of the roughly one-month long menstrual cycle where a female is ovulating and can get pregnant. Now most men don't even know what ovulation is, but that is not why it is called concealed ovulation. Concealed ovulation refers to the incredible fact that both men and women have no clear way of telling when the female is ovulating. In the animal kingdom this is extremely rare. Our female primate cousins have genitals that swell to twice their usual size and turn bright red when they are fertile.[51] It is like a siren announcing to all male primates that she is ready for action. Let's now address extended receptivity. It's far simpler. All it means is that women can have sex throughout their menstrual cycle – whether fertile or not. Again this is rare in the animal kingdom. It means that we can infer that sex does not just serve as a reproductive function. It has another function…

The standard narrative uses these two biological concepts to explain a male's desire to be in a pair-bonding relationship. Remember that concealed ovulation means the male is never sure when the female is fertile. If he knew when she was fertile, he would guard her for this period and leave to impregnate other females when she was not. It is theorized that concealed ovulation evolved to keep the males constantly in a pair-bond with the female.[52] If the male left for even for a moment, they could never be certain that future offspring of the female was theirs. There would be no way of ensuring their resources were not being given to another opportunistic man's child. This would be a disaster according to the theory of natural selection. It is also claimed that extended receptivity exists so females can constantly obtain resources from the man. By being able to have sex throughout her menstrual cycle she could ensure that the man does not seek other sexual encounters. Sex in exchange for resources.

This is the scientific argument for why humans favor marriage. And it's wrong according to Christopher Ryan. Many great thinkers on the podcast believe in the standard model including Steven Pinker, Bret Weinstein, and the great Richard Dawkins but Ryan's argument is more nuanced than you might think and requires some further explanation.

He does not discount this standard narrative entirely. Instead, he argues that the agricultural revolution 10,000 years ago is responsible for the social conditions the standard narrative explains. The advent of agriculture meant the advent of private property. Resources could be collected and invariably power was concentrated to a select few, the males capable of enforcing violence. But as Ryan points out, this is a fraction of the 200,000 years of our evolution as a species. The standard narrative seems at odds with the whole story of human sexuality.

Prior to the agricultural revolution people lived in self-contained groups of hunter-gatherers (foraging tribes). Anthropologists agree these groups operated based on fierce egalitarianism. All resources were shared and an inability to do so was met with serious punishment. It was not because these foragers had read *The Happiness Hypothesis* but rather because it was in their survival interest. The group's wellbeing was the sum of their individual wellbeing. All Ryan's theory does is extend this accepted concept of egalitarianism to sex. It is argued that both males and females would have multiple sexual partners to ensure social cohesion amongst the tribe. Females were sexually promiscuous. As were males. Instead of diplomats, treaties and counseling, tribes used sex as the ultimate tool of peace. It does seem incredible to suggest that females had more sexual freedom in hunter-gather tribes than many women in the 21st century.

Let's examine the evidence for this. It should be noted that Ryan makes many more arguments in his book and podcast but in my view these are not nearly as persuasive. There are two strong arguments:

1. Bonobo research
2. Anthropological data

The bonobo argument stems from the field of primatology, the study of the behavior, biology and evolution of non-human primates. This includes Rogan's fascination with and love of, chimpanzees. Genetically, chimps and bonobos are closer to humans than they are to gorillas or monkeys. In fact, our DNA is so similar to these primates that it varies by only 1.6 percent.[53] Clearly studying these primates is essential to understand the evolution of human sexuality. By observing the mating patterns of one of our closest relatives we can see if the standard narrative of human sexuality holds up.

As Rogan loves to acknowledge on the podcast, chimpanzees are 'savages'. In the wild, they have been observed as violent, deceitful and aggressive animals known to practice infanticide and rape. Conversely, they are also incredibly intelligent creatures who live in elaborate social networks. It would seem they are perfect models for human behavior.

Chimpanzee models of behavior have been used to support the standard narrative of sexuality. This is because their social structures are inherently patriarchal, the male is the undisputed king. Sex is also heavily influenced by status and power. It seems to fit with the idea that marriage evolved so women could get better access to resources from men in a patriarchal society. This is where bonobos cause a huge problem for those who think the above. These primates have only recently been observed in nature and the results are remarkable.

Bonobos are the hippies of our evolutionary past. They are both peaceful and share everything between groups. Caring is sharing when it comes to sex too. Bonobos have sex far more frequently than common chimpanzees and use it to foster social cohesion. Both these species often have sex upwards of five times a day.[54] Female bonobos have multiple partners, as do males. The similarities between bonobos and humans suggest they are even closer to us in behavior than our other primate cousins. Female bonobos, like female humans, have concealed ovulation and can have sex throughout their menstrual cycle. If you recall earlier, this a considerable blow to the parental investment theory. Bonobos have both concealed ovulation and extended receptivity yet they screw prolifically; something is wrong with the standard narrative of sexuality. Ryan does seem to romanticize the 'peace-loving' bonobos at times, and as some scientists point out, the studies have a small sample size and more observation in the wild is needed. They might turn out to just be like their murderous cousins, the chimpanzees. But maybe we were more like the peaceful bonobos in our past. Humans could have used sex as a way of increasing social cohesion between foraging tribes. Perhaps it was the advent of agriculture that brought out in us our chimp cousins' violent, patriarchal tendencies. Sexual promiscuity could have been the default for humans, not marriage.

The anthropological argument provides evidence for this too. There are a handful of communities around the world that have eluded the clutches of globalism. These tribal groups have continued their cultures for thousands of years with minimal influence from the outside world. This allows anthropologists to study these groups including their various sexual practices. If the standard narrative of sexuality is true one would expect males to raise only their child. It turns out they don't usually. Ryan could be accused of cherry-picking but I think the examples he provides, show how weak the standard narrative is. One interesting example comes from the Aché, a tribe living in Paraguay who believe each child has four fathers.[55] This includes a father who 'put it in' and a father who 'provides the child's essence'. One might be excused for thinking this is an outlier but it is not. All around the world anthropologists have provided examples of tribes with different conceptions of parenthood. Many of these groups raise children as a community as opposed to just their biological parents. After all, many don't even know who the biological father is. The standard narrative crumbles here. Why would men care for a child that is not their own?

Ryan's arguments are persuasive. There is a lot of evidence that human sexuality was far more liberal in our evolutionary past than it has been since the establishment of civilizations. Ryan's arguments rely on some cherry-picking and overly romanticizing evidence, and his ideas on sperm competition in his book have been largely discredited.[56] However, his thinking is hugely important. Marriage is an institution that is failing. Almost half of the marriages in the United States end in divorce with an untold number of adulterers worldwide. People with failed marriages are often made to feel like failures and our legal system makes the process of divorce not dissimilar to getting a limb amputated. Women are labeled as 'sluts' for sleeping around, sex is a taboo topic at the family dinner table and kids receive their education from Pornhub.

The takeaway idea from Ryan is not that you should divorce your spouse, or embark on a bachelor's life of casual sex and listening to the Joe Rogan podcast. The takeaway idea is that humans should be more accepting and less judgmental of the innate sexuality we all possess. A lot of our sexual norms are recent social constructs as opposed to hardwired laws of nature. Marriage will work for some and not for others. We should never forget that we are all just sexual primates, monkeys who like to have sex, eat food and occasionally do DMT.

DAVID GOGGINS

06. THE MIND CAN OVERCOME ANYTHING

TOPIC: STOICISM
GUEST: ENDURANCE ATHLETE
PODCAST: #1080, #1212
WHERE TO FIND MORE:
CAN'T HURT ME (BOOK)

The Roman Empire was unforgiving. It had to be – its borders were marked by blood. To the north of the empire were hostile Germanic tribes. To the east, Persians, Parthians and many others who wished death upon the citizens of Rome.

Brutality was a requisite for being alive. Famine and disease would ravage the empire as casually as a wildfire burning through a forest. In 64 A.D., the Great Fire of Rome burnt two-thirds of the entire city, bringing the empire to its knees.

The political landscape was no less kind. A stage for betrayal, hypocrisy and corruption. The ruling senatorial class did everything to maintain the power that had been passed down through their family name. Poison and daggers were accepted methods of coercion.

The way of life in the Roman Empire was harsh and often barbaric. Yet within this furnace of brutality, two great men were forged. Their names were Epictetus and Marcus Aurelius.

Epictetus was a slave, and Marcus Aurelius an emperor. Epictetus was born a slave around 55 A.D., destined for a life of domestic servitude in the ancient town of Hierapolis. He had nothing. Marcus Aurelius had everything. He was often hailed as the greatest emperor of the Roman Empire. He ruled with absolute power from 161 A.D. until 180 A.D. Everything was at his disposal, from a bottomless cup of wine to women from every corner of the empire, and men lining up to sing his praises. These two men could not be further apart in status or power. Yet they were linked by a force stronger than a religious affinity or bloodline. They were linked by a way of life. A philosophy.

A philosophy that was so empowering, it broke the shackles of both a slave and the ego of a ruler. That philosophy was stoicism.

It has been roughly 1,500 years since the fall of the Roman Empire. Today, most men will never see a battlefield, go a night without food, or have a firstborn child die. Most men will not know the life of a slave or an emperor. But the philosophy these two men espoused is now embodied more than ever by one man. A man who has lived a slave's life, but whose achievements are those of a great emperor.

David Goggins doesn't give a fuck about the philosophy of stoicism. He has probably never read *A Manual for Living* by Epictetus or *Meditations* by Marcus Aurelius. Yet he might be the greatest example of the stoic mindset to ever walk the Earth. What makes Goggins remarkable is that his stoicism wasn't learned from textbooks; it was born out of hardship and suffering. Pain was his only teacher. Learning the story of David Goggins will provide evidence that the stoic mindset can change anyone's life. No matter what their life circumstance. Slave or king.

Before we explore the philosophy of stoicism, the question remains – who is David Goggins?

The year is 2006. The heat is almost unbearable in Death Valley, California. Temperatures routinely reach above 113°F (45°C). It is so hot in this stretch of desert that you can fry an egg on the tarmac of the only road that goes through Death Valley. It can only be described as like the surface of Mars, a barren wasteland. But it is also the site of the world's toughest foot race. The Badwater Ultramarathon. The 135-mile (217.2 km) foot race starts at the lowest point in North America, the Badwater Basin. From there, runners traverse three mountain ranges and ascend a cumulative total of 19,000 feet (5,800 meters) finally arriving at one of North America's highest points, the summit of Mt. Whitney. This feat of endurance will be done in extreme heat and a sleep-deprived state. It is a race that people train their entire lives to complete.

David Goggins had never run a marathon before. But he had decided he was going to compete in the 2006 Badwater 135. He called the race organizer and asked if he could compete as the event was strictly invitation only. For good reason – any ill equipped runner would almost certainly injure or kill themselves in the extreme conditions. The organizer of the event, Chris Koster, told Goggins he could not compete unless he had ultramarathon experience, he basically told him to get fucked. Goggins had not run any official marathons, let alone an ultramarathon. But he was equipped to suffer. At this time, he was already an accomplished Navy SEAL in SEAL Team Five who had also attended the United States Army Ranger School and graduated top of his class. These are two of the most elite military units in the world and Goggins had succeeded in both.

With three days' notice, he signed up for his first ultramarathon to qualify for Badwater 135. His burly special forces frame was terribly suited for ultramarathons. Yet he ran 101 miles in 19 hours and 6 minutes. He ran the race with stress fractures in both feet as well as peeing and shitting himself at the finish.

Now Goggins found himself in the heart of Badwater 135. The desert heat, mountainous terrain and delirium from not sleeping broke most of his competitors who were highly experienced distance runners. Goggins' presence at the race was outrageous, a 6ft 2in inexperienced runner with muscles like a powerlifter competing against elite professional ultramarathon runners. Goggins finished fifth overall.

This is a fraction of what David Goggins has achieved. The man has seen combat serving with one of the most elite special force units in the world and after his service becomes a world-class endurance athlete competing in over a hundred of the toughest endurance races. He has cycled, swam and run his way further than most people can drive. He also held the record for most pull-ups in 24 hours (4,030) and has raised millions of dollars for the Special Operations Warrior Foundation. To top it all off, he is the only person who arrived an hour before Joe Rogan at the podcast where he was found doing pull-ups in Rogan's own gym.

David Goggins is the hardest man on the planet.

However, this is not a complete picture of David Goggins. The list of achievements that give him an aura of being a superhuman is misleading. It's easy to assume that a man who can run with broken feet is made of something different from most people. It's easy to say his brain is just wired differently. That he was born with a biological advantage.

David Goggins was born with a broken heart – an undetected congenital heart defect. As you will soon find out, Goggins' life started with both an environmental and biological disadvantage. The only way that he has achieved his feats is through mindset and unknowingly embracing stoic philosophy.

Although Goggins was not born a slave like Epictetus, his situation was arguably worse. His father was a narcissistic pimp who used to own a popular skate rink in Buffalo, New York. His father would inflict serious physical abuse on Goggins, his brother and his mother. The physical abuse was so bad that there were times when he needed to go to the hospital. His father exploited his family, making them work full time in the skate rink for no money which meant Goggins couldn't focus in school as he was exhausted from the previous night's work. He quickly developed a learning disability. When Goggins was eight, the abuse was too much to endure and his mother took her sons and fled. The impoverished single mother took her kids to Brazil, Indiana. They were one of the few African American families in this rural white town and for years, Goggins endured racial abuse. The day he got his first car someone spray painted the N-word on the bonnet.

It seemed like the kid had no hope. He put on weight and became obese as he also battled with bouts of anxiety and depression. Goggins said at the time he blamed the situation on others. He had every right to do so, and I definitely would have. His father had abused him, he had been racially discriminated against and society had largely rejected a minority student with a learning disability. After a few years of trying to make something of himself Goggins enlisted in the Navy. After a few years, he quit. He went back to Brazil, Indiana and started cleaning cockroaches out of restaurants. That was his life.

David Goggins was not a superhero. He was as fallible as any man before him. His traumatic past had left him with many flaws that made success a very unlikely outcome. What was responsible for the metamorphosis of David Goggins? The meteoric rise of a child from poverty and abuse to the toughest man on the planet.

The answer is simply mindset. The stoic mindset. Goggins indirectly discovered the ancient power of stoicism. Founded in Athens in the early 3rd century B.C., the philosophy was one of the first to embody a way of life rather than a set of academic principles. Stoicism was not a theory; it was an existence. Central to the stoic existence is understanding that we don't control, and cannot rely on, external events. We only have control of how we respond to those events. By worrying about things we cannot control we cause ourselves needless worry and angst. We have complete control of how we choose to respond. Our mindset is the only thing we can claim as ours.

> "Remember that foul words or blows themselves are no outrage, but your judgment they are so."[57]

This is what a slave said thousands of years ago. It is the same mindset that has enabled Goggins to achieve impossible human feats. Throughout his life he was subject to external things he had no control over: racism, abuse and poverty. These are all treacherous things that show the inequity of the world we live in. But if Goggins gave up hope because of his hopeless situation, he would, "just be another statistic."[58] Those are his words not mine. The only way Goggins could free himself from his situation was to take total responsibility for the things he could control. His mindset. This liberated him from a life of being enslaved to an external world that was never in his favor. He became a stoic.

The greatest fear of a stoic is that they will make 'chaos of their soul.' They will not live up to their values. They do not fear natural disasters, death or poverty. Their only fear is dying a slave to things outside of their control. Materialism. Greed. Power. The only reason that David Goggins can endure so much suffering is because he is not externally motivated. His drive comes from a deep internal call to test himself to the limits of human capability, to see how far the mind can go.

He constantly talks about going into the depths of your mind. Once you can control your own pain and suffering you can achieve anything. Those who rely on external motivation such as music, other people or motivational YouTube videos will give up the second their internet stops working or they are alone. These people are relying on things that they cannot control.

Those who rely on external things for happiness such as wealth, power and status are destined to be unhappy, enslaved to things they don't have control over. Their happiness can be destroyed by a simple storm that ruins their business or a lover that leaves them. Such things cannot harm the stoic because they do not depend on anything else other than their response. They choose how they feel.

That's what you learn from David Goggins and the philosophy of stoicism. It is easy to label him as an extremist unable to connect with other people. In some ways this is true. His incessant commitment to a stoic mindset has harmed his relationships as he will admit. Not everyone should be like David Goggins. There is obvious value in human relationships. But his unwavering commitment to pushing the limits of human endurance has acted as a canary in a coal mine. He has gone into the mine to check that it is safe for everyone else. He has risked death to show all of us, that we too can achieve anything.

The only enemy will be our own mind.

PAUL STAMETS

07. MUSHROOMS CAN SAVE THE WORLD

TOPIC: NATURE
GUEST: MYCOLOGIST
PODCAST: #1035, #1385
WHERE TO FIND MORE:
MYCELIUM RUNNING (BOOK)

Mushrooms can save the world.

I know it sounds like a bumper sticker on the back of a Volkswagen Beetle. Skepticism is a natural response to such an outlandish idea. Although once you enter the mushroom universe, there is no going back. These fruiting bodies of fungus might hold the answers to our shared survival on Earth. Strap in as we enter the fungus kingdom.

There was a time when almost every human being believed in the supernatural: magic, sorcerers and spirits. Mysticism provided our ancestors with the only answers in a world of questions. Then came the scientific revolution. Our primary tool for understanding the world shifted from story, myth and gods to reason, logic and empirical observation. The sun did not rise because God willed it but because the Earth rotates around its axis, exposing half of our spherical planet to our solar system's star.

Science offered us answers to questions we once did not even know to ask, opening up an entire universe to question and discover. What is dark matter?

Why is there something rather than nothing? Why does quantum mechanics say an electron can be in two places at once?

Sadly, some scientists have disregarded the awe and wonder that arises when examining the universe. Western materialism has condemned anything that even resembles modern-day mysticism. While this is usually a good idea when discussing astrology and Ouija boards, it has come at a cost. Any discussion of the forces of Mother Nature uses language that makes the planet appear dead, a collection of lifeless organisms that are to be examined in Petri dishes under microscopes. It denies the reality that all life on the Earth subsists in a complex state of coexistence. An interconnected web of life.

It is no wonder that the planet is being destroyed when the words we use to describe it are so detached from notions of life and spirit. Dirt is dirt. In reality, a single handful of dirt holds more microbial life than all the plant and vertebrate species in North America.[59] Dirt is not dirt; it is home to a complex ecosystem of microscopic life that humans are yet to fully comprehend. All of this microbial life shares an ancestor with us. The fact that all forms of life are descendants of the same single-cell organism is profoundly mystical; to say otherwise is to deny the shared origins we have with every fungus, plant and animal on the planet. All life started from the same point. From humans to mushrooms. Wonder and mystery exist in every handful of the Earth.

A scientist who has never lost sight of the innate mysticism of nature is Paul Stamets. He is the podcast's most requested guest of all time. It's hard to define Paul Stamets. The most accurate attempt comes from Michael Pollan:

> "Stamets is a visionary emissary from the fungus kingdom [sent] to our world... [and] the possibilities fungi hold for healing the environment will fill you with hope and wonder."

Stamets is undoubtedly of the fungus kingdom, a microbial world that most humans spend little time thinking about. The moment Stamets walks into the Joe Rogan studio, his fungal presence is felt. His hat is made entirely of amadou mushrooms. "This fungus is what the first humans used to transport fire," he says in a voice that you would expect from an elder imparting wisdom round a campfire.

Paul Stamets has an answer about how to save the planet, using mushrooms. The man is one of the world's leading experts in mycology, the study of fungi. He has presented his ideas in popular TED talks and has even been involved in classified U.S. government bio-security projects. This rogue scientist and entrepreneur just might have the answer about how to save the planet from ecological collapse. The answer comes at an appropriate time. Of all current species, 15-37 percent are expected to be dead by 2050 due to human activity.[60] Cutting down forests and burning fossil fuels is having a disastrous impact on many ecosystems. The consequences of this loss of biodiversity are not fully understood. But it doesn't look good. Post-apocalyptic landscapes like those seen in *Mad Max*, *The Road* and *Chernobyl* might be closer than we think.

Take something as small as a honey bee. This insect is experiencing population decimation largely due to pesticides and climate change. In Washington State beekeepers are losing almost 75 percent of their hives.[61] This is happening all around North America. If the honey bee were to completely die out, so too would most agricultural crops. This would be a calamitous issue for the human race. Bees play a vital role in pollinating crops and 35 percent of the crops we eat depend directly on bee pollination.[62] Even something as small as the loss of a bee can trigger a domino effect that collapses our delicate ecosystem leading to agricultural failure. Famine and death usually follow for the poorer people in the world. A fairly bleak outlook for the future of our species.

But there is hope. That hope turns out to be all around you, underneath you.

To understand how mushrooms can save the world we need to step into the mystical world of the natural kingdom. Paul Stamets is our guide. In the forest, you see a bright red mushroom in the distance. You take a step towards it. Unknowingly, you have just stepped on the mushroom itself as this small step impacts over three hundred miles of tangled mycelium.[63] This is the network of roots that are a part of the mushroom. The vast underground networks go in search of nutrients and bring them back to the fruiting body, the mushroom. Mycelium is found in the first few inches of any soil that supports life. It's everywhere; the underground matrix beneath every step you take. The largest living organism is the fungi *Armillaria Ostoyae*, with a mycelium network covering over 2,385 acres.

Mycelium is the 'fungal fabric' that holds nature together. It can disassemble large organic molecules and turn them into simpler forms that nourish the entire ecological community. But it does far more than that. It might even be able to sense when we take a step in the forest. Paul Stamets believes the fungi have some form of consciousness. Each footstep you take into the forest is felt by the 'sentient' mushroom with its vast network of underground information. It might sound crazy but the science he forms his belief on is just that. Crazy.

In 2010, Japanese scientists made a discovery that challenges everything you think you know about nature. They were conducting an experiment on a fungi-like mold called *Physarum polycephalum* where they placed oat flakes on a small, wet mat. The oat flakes were distributed around the mat in the exact configuration of major cities surrounding Tokyo and the mold was placed in the middle. They wanted to see how the mold would grow to find the scattered food source of the oat flakes. At first, the mold appeared to be growing randomly, hoping to stumble across an oat flake by chance. Then something extraordinary happened. The mold self-organized and spread out to form a more efficient network than the Tokyo train network.[64] The mold had figured out the most efficient route to find and exploit the food source. This low life fungus had outperformed human engineers with mathematics and complex data models; it somehow knew how to map its environment more effectively than humans. It intuitively knew where things were.

It's easy to see why Stamets is willing to label fungi as conscious. That claim may be controversial but what is not disputed is how the mycelium acts as an architect for its environment.

Let's say the world did become like Chernobyl. Humans go extinct because of radioactive fallout; there is a mass extinction of animals on a scale the world has never seen. Forests are burnt to ash. Only a few creatures remain.

In this wasteland of nothingness, fungi would begin to grow. The mycelium would stretch its way through the lifeless soil in search of scraps of food. In a matter of weeks, the *Morchella* and *Auricularia* mushrooms would be the first to sprout.[65] The spores from these mushrooms would release fragrances that attract insects. Eventually, smaller mammals would be attracted in the pursuit of insects. Then larger mammals would be attracted in pursuit of smaller mammals. And just like that, the circle of life is restarted and an interconnected ecosystem emerges. The conductor of the orchestra of life was the initial mycelium network which thrived when nothing else could. It steers the course of ecosystems by favoring certain species.[66] This is how we got here. When Earth's surface was inhospitable, teeming with volcanic activity, it was fungi that stayed alive. Discoveries of fossilized mushrooms show they are one of the oldest living organisms dating back over 1.3 billion years. For millions and millions of years, their mycelium networks were refined, becoming more and more effective at servicing the food chain and controlling the environment. The influence that mushrooms have had on the world today cannot be overstated.

All mushrooms are powerful, not just the magic ones.

But how can they save the world? Paul Stamets is like an ancient sage who conjures potions not known to the common man, the master of mushrooms who uses mycelium as his main ingredient. Through his often ad hoc strategy of harnessing the properties of these fungal networks, Stamets is helping to save the world. Take the bees for example. Stamets found out how to use fungi to stabilize bee populations and prevent their mass extinction. He is the author of one of the most viewed *Nature* articles of all time: *Extracts of Polypore Mushroom Mycelia Reduce Viruses in Honey Bees.*[67] For the skeptics, *Nature* is one of the most reputable scientific journals in the world. This sage is mainstream, alternative and everything in between.

Stamets knew that fungi produce chemicals which can be used to fight virus and bacteria in humans. He had a revelation. He had worked for years as a lumberjack, and remembered seeing bears leave their claw marks on trees. This would lead to fungi growing out from the exposed bark where the claws had slashed the tree. More bees would now approach the tree. Stamets hypothesized that the bees were using the fungi in the same way humans used mushrooms – for antibacterial properties. He was right. He found a certain strain of mycelium that helped to protect the bees against the virus that was ravaging their community. He is saving the bees and indirectly all of us.

This is a part of a larger idea. Mushrooms provide a path to save the planet. We need to use them to restore balance to ecological communities that are being destroyed. Mycelium can be used by humans as a tool that has become a master of maintaining the equilibrium of ecosystems over a billion years.

This concept is called mycorestoration. These ancient mycelium networks have shown incredible promise in various fields from filtering toxins out of the environment, offering safe alternatives to pesticides, and making farming sustainable and profitable. Mushrooms really can save the planet.

Take for instance the power of mycelium to filter toxins. Years back, Stamets bought a small farm in Washington. The livestock on the property, and on those surrounding his farm, were causing a huge problem as their feces were not being drained properly. The inadequate drainage systems led to a buildup of toxic fecal coliform pollution and the shellfish industry in the nearby inlet was under threat. This led to Sheriffs visiting his property – and all of his neighbors – to tell them they had to install new septic tanks within two years or vacate the land. Stamets had another idea. He managed to use mushrooms and their mycelium nets as natural filtration systems. The government inspectors returned, found no new septic tank and were amazed that Stamet's property was better than any other they had examined.[68] The mycelium was filtering out the microbial pollution. Nature could be exploited for the benefit of the entire ecosystem. This is, after all, what mushrooms have been doing long before humans polluted the Earth.

This is just one example of the many ways mycorestoration is currently being used to disrupt many commercial industries. Stamets has dozens of patents. Some of which are ideas that could potentially revolutionize the agricultural industry in the next decade. The power of these ancient mycelium networks is not to be understated.

Paul Stamets is undoubtedly eccentric. The mushroom oracle thinks more creatively than most people would after ingesting a particular type of mushroom. His speculation about mycelium's consciousness might be strange to some, but it is more of an opinion based on his research than an opinion that guides his research. The man is a scientist above all else and his work has adhered to the scientific method to prove his underlying suspicions.

Mushrooms really can save the world.

JORDAN PETERSON

08. STAND STRAIGHT WITH YOUR SHOULDERS BACK

TOPIC: PHILOSOPHY
GUEST: PSYCHOLOGIST
PODCAST: #877, #958, #1006, #1070, #1164 +
WHERE TO FIND MORE:
12 RULES FOR LIFE (BOOK)

The future is unpredictable. If you asked someone in 2014 who the next most famous public intellectual would be, they probably would have said a climate scientist or maybe even an AI expert.

No one could have predicted what came next. A softly spoken clinical psychologist from the University of Toronto who regularly quotes Nietzsche, the Bible and psychology studies became an international phenomenon; his name was Jordan Peterson. Hordes of disillusioned young men consumed any content they could find as videos with Peterson quickly amassed millions of views. Peterson went on talk shows, podcasts and lectures where his articulate and clear message resonated with an even larger audience. Besides Elon Musk, he is the most popular guest on the Joe Rogan podcast of all time.

What was his message? It was not about rock music, psychedelics or rebelling against the system. His message was about assuming personal responsibility. The psychology professor was making a plea for young men to accept responsibility in life and the message was being consumed like crack cocaine. How did we reach a point in our society that this traditional message has become a counterculture view?

In 2015, Peterson was a relatively unknown professor. At this time, Canada was attempting to pass legislation that would mandate the use of compelled speech. It would be unlawful not to use gender-neutral pronouns such as ze/zei to refer to a transgender person. Peterson went viral in a video where he was confronted by an angry mob of protesters in reaction to his criticism of the legislation.[69] Calmly, he explained that while he would call students by their preferred pronoun if asked, mandating forced speech was a dangerous path to go down. As a scholar Peterson had read extensively on the horrors of the Soviet Union and was acutely aware of how a society could transition from order to chaos. Without upholding the right to free speech, a democracy could descend into the tyrannical reign of a dictator who establishes forced labor camps for those that disagree. That might sound like a bit of a stretch but it is precisely what happened in Soviet Russia, the Gulags are not just a video game map, they were forced Siberian labor camps that killed over a million dissenters just eighty years ago. That's one lifetime away.

The need to preserve freedom of speech and free academic inquiry is a more serious issue than you think. And the threats our society face are as real as ever. A toxic ideology is brewing in universities worldwide and has already made its way to corporate and public spheres. This ideology is postmodernism; Peterson calls it the "new skin of Marxists." What could he possibly mean by that?

Peterson is referring to a large body of academics with inclinations to the communist writings of Karl Marx. In the West, communism went out of fashion in academic circles in the seventies. For good reason, the abject failure of communism and its involvement in the deaths of millions made it impossible to openly support such an ideology. Some Western academics used a sleight of hand and replaced Marxism with a subtler ideology, postmodernism. The ideology is responsible for much of the identity politics we see today. Postmodernists believe that there are two classes of people, the oppressor and the victim. They believe that all institutions are powerful structures that oppress the masses, with some calling for radical change even if it involves reverse discrimination.[70] In their view, the white male is the guiltiest oppressor of all, the patriarchal villain of history. This is the destructive message being taught to young men, the majority of whom have no economic privilege, that they are the problem with society.

So what is Jordan Peterson's message? His message is more than just assuming personal responsibility and walking with your shoulders back. It is a message that calls upon the individual to understand how the world works before seeking to make it better, even if the truth is uncomfortable. Here is why you should stand straight with your shoulders back.

The world is not fair. The wealthiest one percent of the world's population owns more than half of the world's wealth. In America, the top 10 percent own 77 percent of the wealth. People are rightfully upset about the gross income inequality that exists in our society. But to blame it solely on capitalism is foolish for one reason. The Pareto distribution. Any field that is based on human productivity follows what is called a Pareto distribution. This refers to a probability distribution where a tiny percentage of people account for almost all the output. It applies to books, music, movies, farming, business, politics and the list goes on. For example, let's say there are 100 million people who listen to podcasts each month. Then let's say there are a million podcasts to choose from. It does not follow a normal distribution or bell curve where most podcasts get around 100,000 views and then on the extreme ends a handful of podcasts get no views and a handful get millions of views. It doesn't work like that because podcasts require creative output so a Pareto distribution governs it. Of the million podcasts, almost all will have less than a hundred views while only a handful will have all the listeners. Think of all the people you know who have podcasts and compare them to the Joe Rogan podcast. The same goes for book sales, music and even work, a handful of people produce all the songs we listen to, all the books we read and complete all the work done in the office despite the fact there are plenty of writers, singers and workers. It doesn't matter what system you have, be it communism, socialism or capitalism the same rule applies. The distribution is by no means fair.

Why is the Pareto distribution important? Because this is a fundamental reality of any system that requires human capital. Systems that have sought to redistribute resources without acknowledging this law of nature have failed. An example Peterson uses is Soviet Russia. The Pareto distribution applied to farming where a handful of peasant farmers had accumulated wealth by being the most productive. The communist intellectuals thought the less successful peasant farmers should take over these productive farms as the successful farmers were sent to die at the Gulags. The result was catastrophic. Six million people died of famine in Ukraine as inefficient farmers could not produce enough food.

This is the first lesson that Peterson teaches, the world is by no means fair and success is concentrated in the hands of a few. Does this mean we should all give up and accept that people have more resources than us? On the contrary, it means we must realize what the stakes of the game are; everything is in the balance. It is a call to switch on and beat the system to make it better for everyone else. Simply complaining about the system will do nothing, we must understand it to change it. We all exist in these dominance hierarchies and our place on this ladder influences every aspect of our life from who we mate with to our body posture. Some people prefer to shy away from this reality labeling any discussion of dominance hierarchies as 'oppressive.' Only by acknowledging their existence can one hope to change their situation. This simple idea is about how to change your position in the dominance hierarchy.

A dominance hierarchy exists when members of a social group interact and create a ranking system. The term is commonly used in biology for a hierarchy that governs social groups of mammals. Although Peterson does not reference wolves in great depth they are the clearest example of a dominance hierarchy. Each wolf pack consists of an alpha male and an alpha female. They are generally the only two wolves who mate in the pack. There are then several beta wolves. They are the next in line and will challenge the alpha wolf when they sense weakness. Finally, there are the omega wolves, usually an omega male and female. They are at the bottom of the pecking order and are sometimes killed by the pack when play-fighting goes too far. They exist in a constant state of terror as they must submit to every other wolf in the pack. While no one disputes the existence of these dominance hierarchies in the animal kingdom, we sometimes forget they exist in human societies too. Obviously, there is more complexity in human social networks. Peterson makes no attempt at justifying the rather illusory concept of an alpha male – people who are high up in dominance hierarchies have much less to do with aggression and testosterone than you might think.

First let's look at lobsters. This is Peterson's famous example in his book, *12 Rules for Life*. It might seem strange to compare humans to lobsters. But we forget that we evolved from a common ancestor around 360 million years ago. Evolution tends to build upon systems already there and much of our wiring traces its origins to these ancient crustaceans. They have a comparatively simple nervous system which has enabled scientists to study them in great depth. Despite the obvious difference that lobsters are crustaceans that live in the sea, they also share some common environmental features with us. They too must find a neighborhood to live in, food to eat and a partner to mate with. As a result of this competitive social structure lobsters have developed innate defensive behaviors that can be observed in a laboratory. When lobsters compete for shelter they will dance back and forward with their claws raised while simultaneously deploying special jets under their eyes. This liquid that comes from these jets contains chemicals that alert the other lobster to its competitor's size, health, and mood.[71] Usually, this will provide the inferior lobster with an opportunity to retreat from combat and not risk conflict's devastating effects. However, if the two are evenly matched, the creatures will continue dominance displays until all-out combat ensues. The price of combat for lobsters is immense. The lobster that loses the battle will quite literally have its brain dissolve and a new subordinate brain takes its place. Furthermore, its serotonin levels will decrease significantly. As serotonin levels are responsible for postural flexion, the defeated lobster's weak body language will signal to all around it that it is of low status. It will be unable to find a desirable place to live on the ocean floor as it is too weak to engage in competition with other male lobsters.

The champion lobster in comparison will have an increase in serotonin and a decrease in octopamine.[72] This means the lobster is chemically confident and struts around the ocean's most desired real estate. With male lobsters constantly competing for dominance this system enables female lobsters to outsource the problem of mating to the machine calculations of these dominance hierarchies. All the females will try to choose the champion lobster in the best location as this means he is the strongest and most fit for reproduction. It's not too dissimilar to a world where a big house on the beach sends a similar signal. We don't need to know the person who lives in the house to know they are likely a high status individual at the top of their relevant dominance hierarchy.

The winner of the lobster's ancient dominance hierarchy has the entire world at their crustacean feet. Humans' social structures are undoubtedly more complex than that of the lobster as many who criticize Peterson point out. But humans are more similar to lobsters than you may think, it's the same reason that Prozac, a drug for human depression works on lobsters too. [73]

These ancient systems of status and hierarchies exist within us. Each human has a primordial calculator monitoring their position in society. Peterson uses an arbitrary scale of one to ten for the sake of argument (one being the highest status and ten being the lowest status). People watch how they are treated to inform where they are on this scale and your position in the hierarchy will have observable biological impacts on your entire body. Those who are a ten (the lowest social status) will exist in a state of hyper-arousal which means the body will shut down the immune system to focus on an immediate fight or flight response. As a result, they are significantly more susceptible to cancer, dementia and obesity.[74] Furthermore, they will have the lowest serotonin levels and are far more likely to engage in impulsive pleasure-seeking behaviors (drugs and alcohol). Drugs and alcohol are more likely to result in addictions because of low self-esteem and lack of social support. Addiction will only further cripple the individual. This is called a negative feedback loop; it's like a negative accelerator that makes things go from bad to horrible in days or months.

The opposite is true for those at the top of a dominance hierarchy. They will operate with high levels of serotonin and low levels of cortisol (stress hormone). As their fight or flight response is not constantly activated this enables the prefrontal cortex to make more long term decisions. Gratification can be delayed in the short term for much bigger long term rewards. For example, studying to obtain good grades to get a good job is far easier. This is a positive feedback loop, it's a like a positive accelerator where things only keep getting better.

It is imperative to understand that human dominance hierarchies are brutal. They are systematically reinforced by feedback loops. They are not governed by rules of equality with all people starting at the bottom of the ladder. We were all born on different rungs of the ladder of life, you do not just not climb one rung at a time. You can fall straight to the bottom and never get back up. You can start at the bottom and never progress at all. But there is hope.

Peterson explains that these systems are based on how people perceive us. It is people's perception that subconsciously informs us of our place in these dominance hierarchies. Think of an ineffectual person who walks in public as if they don't want to be seen. Hunched over. Head down. Nervously touching their neck. People perceive them as weak and will treat them accordingly. You must walk through the world with purpose. Shoulders back. Head up. Even if you still feel without purpose, doing so and making it a habit will change the way hundreds of people interact with you each day. Those looks of disdain on the subway commute can become a silent acknowledgment of your existence. Such a simple habit has the propensity to alter your body's biochemistry, which is enough to get the positive feedback loop working in your favor.

When a lobster who has just lost a battle is injected with serotonin it instantly adopts a confident posture and moves with its former confidence. It is treated with respect as if it had never lost the battle at all. The world is not a fair place and only when we understand how the world works, can we walk with our shoulders back and go about changing it.

MICHAEL POLLAN

09. PSYCHEDELICS CAN BE USEFUL

TOPIC: PSYCHEDELICS
GUEST: JOURNALIST
PODCAST: #1121
WHERE TO FIND MORE:
HOW TO CHANGE YOUR MIND (BOOK)

ALICE STARTED TO HER FEET, FOR IT FLASHED ACROSS HER MIND THAT SHE HAD NEVER BEFORE SEEN A RABBIT WITH EITHER A WAISTCOAT-POCKET, OR A WATCH TO TAKE OUT OF IT, AND BURNING WITH CURIOSITY, SHE RAN ACROSS THE FIELD AFTER IT, AND FORTUNATELY WAS JUST IN TIME TO SEE IT POP DOWN A LARGE RABBIT-HOLE UNDER THE HEDGE.

Alice's Adventures in Wonderland by Lewis Carroll

Alice went down the rabbit hole. It is quite remarkable that a seven-year-old girl was willing to follow a talking rabbit down a deep dark hole without any anxiety. Her curiosity was greater than fear, a formula for any adventure. The story of Alice in Wonderland has been adopted by the psychedelic movement with many claiming Lewis Carroll wrote it under the influence of psychedelic drugs. This does not appear to be true.[75]

Psychedelics are a class of prohibited psychoactive substances that produce changes in perception, mood and cognitive processes. The category includes LSD, psilocybin, ayahuasca and mescaline. All can produce hallucinations and an altered state of consciousness (one in which talking rabbits could very well exist). Although Lewis Carroll may not have taken any of these drugs, the story of Alice in Wonderland does capture the essence of the movement. A group of people willing to go down the rabbit hole of their own minds. An adventure where curiosity overcomes the fear of never returning – losing one's sanity.

Why would anyone want to go down the rabbit hole of psychedelics? The prospect of losing touch with reality is easily the greatest fear I have; it's definitely not Rogan's. The podcast has infamously popularized the psychedelic drug DMT. It is always funny when Joe asks the greatest minds of the 21st century if they have tried the most powerful psychedelic drug on the planet. They usually say no, including the eighty-year-old biologist, Richard Dawkins. Rogan would speak of his experiences with these substances with great respect, almost as if they were some teacher who had imparted great insight to him. I was skeptical. To someone who knew nothing about the topic, it sounded like the kind of thing someone into alchemy would say at a card reading convention.

Then Michael Pollan came on the podcast. Pollan is a professor of practice of non-fiction at Harvard University. He is one of the greatest science journalists alive, but more importantly, he is sixty years old. Old enough to be my dad. His age was important because of the provocative title of his new book, *How to Change your Mind: The New Science of Psychedelics*. If anyone could lead me on an objective exploration of this topic, it was a veteran science writer with a nose for bullshit.

Just like Alice, I was ready to go down the rabbit hole.

Pollan's 400-page book skillfully weaves a narrative of the history of psychedelics, neuroscience and his personal exploration with these substances.

His discussion of the ancient use of these drugs reminded me of a trip I took to Belize in Central America. By trip, I mean holiday not a journey into the fourth dimension with talking pyramids and frogs. San Ignacio, is a small town amid the jungles of Belize. The jungles grow on a water-soluble limestone formation called Karst. This gives rise to an intricate cave system that runs beneath the jungle like a labyrinth of dark interconnected tunnels. Thousands of years ago, the Mayans who lived in these jungles thought these caves were portals to the underworld. We descended into the mouth of a deep dark cave called the Actun Tunichil Muknal. The system of caves was so vast that anyone without a torch would almost certainly be trapped beneath the jungle forever, stuck in both metaphorical and literal hell. The Mayans would descend into the 'underworld' and conduct religious ceremonies in the depths of the cave. This ceremony included taking psychedelic substances that had spiritual significance in ancient Mayan culture.[76] Our guide told us their torches would make them see shadows dancing on the walls of the cave, which to their intoxicated eyes must have only been one thing, the Gods. In summary, they were descending into a maze of pitch-black underground tunnels holding fire torches while under the influence of psychoactive compounds. They make Alice going down the rabbit hole sound like the child's story it is.

Psychedelics have been used by ancient cultures for thousands of years. This has been well documented; from the Amazonian tribes' use of ayahuasca, and American Indians' use of the Peyote Cactus (contains mescaline).[77] The use of these compounds back then was predominately for spiritual and religious purposes, often in ceremonies led by a Shaman – usually a respected elder of the tribe or some form of healer. It should be of little surprise that these cultures used psychedelic compounds, they were after all sourced from the natural world. When smoked, the Sonoran Desert Toad's venom contains the DMT molecule,[78] and psilocybin is found in certain mushrooms that populate forest floors. Yes, a schedule one drug, the same category as heroin, can be found on a forest floor near you. This fact was somewhat of a turning point for me. How was an edible mushroom that caused visual hallucinations for about three hours the same as heroin? Psychedelics are some of the only drugs with non-addictive properties where it is virtually impossible to die from an overdose.[79] Why were these drugs so vilified? It didn't make sense.

It only makes sense when the history of psychedelics in the West is explained. Michael Pollan provides a full exploration of this turbulent history which is so engrossing it should be made into a motion picture. For the sake of time, I will stick to the highlights. Albert Hofmann was the first man to try LSD in 1938. He synthesized the new chemical and then accidentally ingested it. Let's just say he struggled to ride his bike home from work that day. After the world's first LSD trip, Hofmann was convinced this powerful chemical would have some clinical benefit. Although he had no idea what that benefit might be. As a result, he gave the chemical free of charge to any research institution willing to find out. Research into psychedelics began – although no one outside of a select few researchers and mental health professionals knew of its existence. This all changed in 1955. A JP Morgan bank executive with a passion for mycology (the study of fungi) ventured to Mexico. Through his research, he heard of a mysterious mushroom used by the indigenous population to have hallucinations. He tried what would later become the 'magic mushroom'. A newspaper article about the bank executive's experience with the mushroom went 'viral' in an age before the internet.[80] The public was captivated by the idea of a mind-altering mushroom. However, they had a long way to go before they were a part of the mainstream.

The story only gets wilder. Al Hubbard was born poor in rural Kentucky and dropped out of school by the third grade. In his lifetime, he worked with bootleggers to smuggle alcohol, supplied uranium during the war, became a millionaire from a boat chartering business, worked for the CIA and is responsible for popularizing LSD. Hubbard believed that everyone in America should be exposed to the chemical for its profound spiritual insight – he was a conservative Christian after all. It would have been difficult to conjure up such a peculiar biography unless you were under the influence. His strategy was to give it to the elites – writers, politicians, scientists and spiritual leaders. He hoped it would trickle down into the wider population from there. A fucked up version of trickle-down economics. Although there were many other forces at play, Al Hubbard was a primary force for kick-starting the first wave of psychedelics in the West.

Writers, poets and actors went to work. Aldous Huxley, Paul McCartney, Cary Grant and Allen Ginsberg were a few of the prominent figures who lit the fuse on psychedelics and the counter-culture of the 1960s.

Scientists had also been at work and for far longer. Early research was reporting very promising signs of psychedelics as a therapeutic agent. The drugs were showing an unheard of effectiveness in treating addiction, depression and anxiety. Some alcoholics were going into complete remission from a single session with LSD. The psychiatric community was ecstatic; a new revolution had arrived.

Unfortunately, public exuberance for these drugs grew faster than the scientific research. Disgraced Harvard professor Timothy Leary famously said to America's youth, "Turn on, tune in, drop out." Leary was overtly encouraging students to experiment with psychedelic drugs. America's youth happily obliged. This was beyond reckless as the scientific evidence involved trained professionals administering pure forms of the drugs to participants in controlled environments. In contrast, Leary indirectly encouraged people to take 'bootleg' versions of the drug, and often in already highly stimulating environments such as music festivals. It is now well known that psychedelics can trigger a psychosis in young adolescents with a genetic predisposition for schizophrenia. As a result, a small number of young people were showing up in hospital wards around America. The media, of course, hyperbolized this risk and sent America into a moral panic. People were convinced psychedelics were a one-way ticket to insanity. All research was stopped. Psychedelics became a schedule one drug.

It turns out that a lot of other things can trigger a psychosis for people with a genetic predisposition for schizophrenia. Parents getting a divorce. Moving out of home. And marijuana. The moral panic about psychedelics led to their genuine benefit being overlooked because of a dramatically overstated, albeit real, threat.

Michael Pollan is at the center of a second wave of psychedelics now rippling through Western society. Researchers across the U.S. and Europe have begun to re-explore these drugs in a clinical context. The dark ages of psychedelic research are over. The results all seem to vindicate the 1960s research; a psychiatric revolution is underway.

The most impressive results are from the use of psychedelics in the treatment of addiction. In this field, a smoking habit is known to be a notoriously difficult to kick. Incredibly, preliminary findings have shown that administering psilocybin in just one session can lead to long-term smokers abstaining from cigarettes. The study at John Hopkins University showed that of fifteen participants, 67 percent had abstained from smoking for one whole year after their first session with psilocybin.[81] There is no other treatment that comes even remotely close to this level of success for ending addiction. Indeed, studies of the use of psychedelics to curb addiction have been replicated multiple times with great success in areas such as treating alcoholism.[82]

The therapeutic benefit does not stop just at addiction. Psychedelics have had remarkable success in treating depression and anxiety. One particularly interesting study done by New York University gave psilocybin to terminally ill cancer patients to test its effect on their existential fear of dying. These are patients who are experiencing unimaginable angst as they confront their mortality. It would seem anything that could alleviate their suffering would be helpful. The results are paradigm-shifting. Over 80 percent of cancer patients showed clinically significant reductions in anxiety and depression levels after only one session with psilocybin.[83] Somehow this mysterious compound had helped them come to terms with dying.

Studies have also administered psychedelics to healthy people. The results are equally remarkable as half of the volunteers said their single exposure to psilocybin was the most important spiritual experience of their life. When you consider the breadth of human experience, it seems pretty extraordinary that one afternoon with a psychedelic substance could be as powerful an experience as bringing new life into the world or falling in love for the first time.

Why are these compounds so powerful and how can Western society harness them? Michael Pollan has some answers. Without going into too much detail, the basic theory proposed by some neuroscientists is as follows.[84] The world is a chaotic place. Sensory information would overwhelm us if we did not have a structured way of processing it. This is what the brain does. It turns chaos into order. As we get older we get more efficient at processing information; there is more structure and rigidity in our minds. This is beneficial as it makes adults more productive as they are less distracted by irrelevant sensory inputs. The brain of a child is very different. They seem to be in constant awe of the world and are very easily distracted. Their brains are yet to be efficient at processing only the relevant sensory input and disregarding the rest. It's the reason that childhood summers last for eternity whereas adults blink and the seasons have changed. Time goes by quickly when you have learned how to process stimuli in the world efficiently. This is disadvantageous for many reasons and the novel perspective of a child is often overlooked – yet it's that which allows them to see things that adults do not. They are free from rigid and structured ways of thinking, which allows them to solve certain problems in a more creative way than adults. It isn't my opinion, it's science. Researchers have found some types of problems that a child is better at solving than an adult.

When the brain of someone on psychedelics is monitored, brain activity shows something very interesting. Compared to a baseline, the brain is communicating with parts that it never usually connects with. It is a completely novel state of consciousness where the typical rigid patterns of thinking dissolve. This is why researchers liken the brain of someone tripping to a child.[85] It lets people perceive things through a child's eyes, enabling a flood of sensory information to flow in while the typical rigid patterns of thinking are gone. These are the rigid patterns of thinking that are often responsible for addiction, depression and anxiety. This is why the drugs are so effective at treating these conditions.

As ancient civilizations knew, in certain contexts, psychedelics can have tremendous benefits. A professional clinician (basically just a modern Shaman) and a safe environment are the essential parts for a positive experience with these powerful chemicals. They could not only assist in the mental health epidemic in the West but could also aid healthy people in their day to day lives by providing a profound experience similar to those reported by the John Hopkins volunteers.

There is another benefit for Western culture. If, like Alice, most adults saw a talking rabbit they would probably rush to the psychiatrist and ask for a very high dose of Thorazine. Obviously it's just a story, but the same awe and curiosity that led Alice to follow the rabbit is the same openness to experience required for the most ingenious discoveries to be made. It's also the same trait that is needed for the best jokes to be told and the wisest words to be written. Creativity is an essential ingredient in the modern world and it is under attack from spreadsheets, schedules and seminars. The adult world is filled with close-mindedness and habitual ways of thinking, now more than ever.

There is something immeasurably valuable in seeing the world through the eyes of a child or someone on psychedelics. These chemicals offer a window into a way of seeing problems with a novel perspective. The founder of Apple, Steve Jobs, credits taking LSD as one of the most profound experiences of his life. He summarizes the curiosity of the psychedelics movement best with:

> "Older people sit down and ask, what is it, but the boy asks, what can I do with it."

Well you can do a lot of things with a mushroom...

NICK BOSTROM

10. THE WORLD MIGHT BE A COMPUTER SIMULATION

TOPIC: ARTIFICIAL INTELLIGENCE
GUEST: PHILOSOPHER
PODCAST: #1350
WHERE TO FIND MORE:
SUPERINTELLIGENCE (BOOK)

Do you want to take the red pill or the blue pill?

Choose the blue pill, you will forget this chapter and believe anything you want to believe. Take the red pill and you will see how deep the rabbit hole goes. "Remember, all I am offering is the truth," said Morpheus to Neo.

This is from the most famous scene in *The Matrix*. Neo is given a choice between ignorance or truth. The one catch is that once he takes the red pill, there is no turning back, he must accept the reality of his existence no matter how disturbing it is, even if the reality is that he lives in a computer simulation run by malevolent machines. What if you too lived in a simulation? Would you want to know?

This chapter is a metaphorical red pill, it offers a candid perspective of what might be the true nature of existence. Even if that existence is not what we want it to be. Proceed at your own risk.

You are Neo. The protagonist of your own world. Morpheus is Nick Bostrom, the guest on the Joe Rogan podcast who invented the argument about why we might be living in a computer simulation. He is also an expert on artificial intelligence, a professor of philosophy at the University of Oxford and founder of the Future of Humanity Institute. He is the perfect guide to take you down the rabbit hole and question if you are in a computer simulation.

There are three possibilities. One of which, logically, must be true. The first possibility is that humans go extinct before they reach a 'posthuman' stage.[86] The second possibility is it's very unlikely that 'posthuman' civilizations would have the resources to run many complex simulations of their evolutionary history. The third possibility is that we are almost certainly living in a computer simulation.

This argument is going to require some unpacking. The first possibility is quite simple; it involves some future catastrophe that wipes out our entire species before reaching a technological maturity where simulations are possible. Between meteorites, volcanic eruptions, nuclear warfare and artificial intelligence itself, it's not hard to imagine something that could pose an existential risk to civilization. We may simply never become that advanced because something really bad happens.

But if we do manage to avoid a global catastrophe, then the likelihood we are living in a simulation is exceedingly high.

Here's why you are probably simulated.

If you're like me, you feel fairly stupid sometimes – incapable of remembering names or using my phone calculator to do basic math. Being human is to feel dumb a lot of the time. And there's a lot of topics we can feel dumb about: aeronautical engineering, quantum mechanics, coding computers – the list goes on. We are made to feel stupid because humans are exceptionally good at becoming specialists with narrow domain knowledge. That's how the economy works; people get skills in a very narrow field and then charge money for their expertise. This makes us feel dumb because there are people who know more than us in literally everything we could imagine, there are even people better than us at imagining.

But there is actually no reason for you to feel stupid as the human brain is currently the most advanced form of intelligence of any living organism. It can reason in a range of domains; a human can play a game of chess then write a poem then solve an equation then decode social cues of an upset spouse mad they didn't take out the trash and did stupid shit all day. Most people might only be able to do all of these things at a basic level, but the fact they can apply their cognition to a range of fields is the very thing that makes humans special. Human brains are a multi-tool of intelligence. But you are not going to be special for much longer, something else is coming.

Artificial intelligence.

Although we might not be special for much longer, we do live in special times. No other human beings in history have experienced such exponential growth of technology and the economy. The world economy took 909 years to double for farming society while it takes roughly 6.3 years for industrial society.[87] This is unprecedented. As a result, humans will experience significant technological advancements in a single lifetime. A clear example of this exponential growth in technology is 'Moore's Law'. The law states simply that since the conception of the computer in 1970, processing power has doubled on average every two years.[88] Exponentials lead to a rate of growth that the human mind struggles to comprehend. It's why in 1980, the world's best hard drive could store 2.5 GB, was the size of a refrigerator, and cost $142,000.[89]

This once state of the art technology couldn't even store one Adam Sandler movie. Now, computers can store databases of every movie commercially available into hard drives the size of your hand. Change is rapid.

Artificial intelligence is benefiting from this exponential rise in computer processing power. Each year, achievements that were previously impossible for AI systems are being surpassed. People once viewed chess as the ultimate test of human intelligence. That was until 1997 when an AI system beat the world's best player, Garry Kasparov. Although it wasn't checkmate for humans, as there were still more complicated games where AI systems could not beat human players.

The game of Go is an ancient Chinese board game with simple rules but immense complexity. There are more legal positions on the board than there are atoms in the universe. This is far beyond what any computer is remotely capable of processing. Instead of processing power, the game requires human intuition, creativity and strategic thinking. Many believed it would take decades for AI systems to beat humans at Go.

They were wrong.

In 2016, Google's DeepMind AI program, AlphaGo, beat the 18-time world champion Lee Sadol at the game of Go. It was a landmark victory; the machines had arrived. Human players were now inferior to machines in all strategy board games.[90] But what is more frightening is how AlphaGo managed to beat the world champion. The program did not study a single human game nor did it require human intervention.

It learned to be the greatest in the world entirely by itself. The AI system used something called a neural network. A neural network is basically computer software inspired by how our biological neurons work. Researchers plagiarized from nature. The neural network initially knew nothing about the game. It learned by playing millions of games against itself, constantly updating the neural network. The power of the AI's search algorithms and computer processing means this learning takes place over a couple of days. It's like leaving a child in a room with a violin and watching them emerge just a few days later as an old man who has mastered the instrument. This is called 'deep learning' and AI researchers are expanding their targets. They have shown success in winning more sophisticated role playing games using these methods. Now it's only a matter of time before AI uses 'deep learning' to master the world us humans occupy. Reality.

Nothing so far explains how we might be living in a computer simulation. All we know is that there are some super smart AI programs out there that can self-learn. How is this relevant to us being simulated?

There is something looming on the horizon. An event which has the capacity to change every single aspect of your life. It is called the intelligence explosion. If this event happens, the technology available to humans will exceed anything we have imagined. Only once we understand the magnitude of the explosion to come, does the prospect of our whole world being simulated seem possible.

A survey of leading experts in AI-related fields shows that 50 percent of experts believe human-level machine intelligence will be attained by 2050.[91]

This is not AI that beats you in chess or other board games; this is AI that is the same as you at everything. It's AI capable of writing poems, solving equations and socially reading humans. Most importantly, it's AI capable of designing machines, machines that are better than itself.

This is why experts such as Bostrom speculate a future event greater than the agricultural or industrial revolution. The intelligence explosion. Once AI reaches a certain level, it will be capable of self-improvement leading to unparalleled machine superintelligence. Machines will design smarter machines that then design even smarter machines. Machines will rapidly eclipse human intelligence. The growth is exponential.

Consider this, our brains have billions of axons that communicate (with action potentials) at speeds of 120 m/s or less. We might be the smartest creature on the planet but this is incredibly slow. The laws of physics could allow billions of axons to communicate at the speed of light, 300,000 m/s.[92] Bostrom shows that with these speeds it would be possible for machine intelligence to read every single book on the planet in minutes or it could write a PHD thesis in seconds. AI could create technology beyond that which even science fiction writers thought possible.

Now we have an idea of the technological power available to future humans, let's look at how these future people could simulate us. The entire human brain could be replicated digitally. There is nothing in the laws of physics which suggests it can't. This process is referred to as a 'whole brain emulation'. Bostrom identifies three prerequisites for this to be possible:

1. Advancements in brain scanning.
2. Translation of this scanning into data that accounts for a three-dimensional model of the brain with relevant neurocomputational inputs.
3. Simulation hardware powerful enough to reconstruct this data input.[93]

If that sounded like an instruction manual too complicated to read, don't worry, it is. All you need to take away is that there will come a time when brain scans will detect everything that is going on in our heads. They will be able to see in real-time when a neuron fires, what structures are activated, and when and how they are all connected. This data can then be input into a powerful machine that simulates our brain's exact inputs, digitally. A brain could be simulated.

When you kill a character in a video game you don't feel bad. That's because the player isn't a conscious being; they are an arrangement of pixels coded to do certain things. They don't think like us. They can't love, reason or hate. But what will happen when the technology reaches a level where our entire brains are replicated digitally. Would feelings of love not be available to these digital brains? Digital brains that have the exact same brain wiring as us, the same flaws and strengths. If every dendrite, cell axon and neural message is the same it is almost impossible to argue they would not think like us.

This is the assumption of Bostrom's argument, that if the brain was replicated exactly then the same subjective experience of consciousness would arise.[94] Many people would disagree with this, favoring the idea that what makes us human is our soul. Something that can't be recreated by a machine. An intangible part of our being.

But if these simulations exist in the future, they will be capable of language. Think of their first sentence. What if the digital brain says, "Where am I?" You can't help but feel that the digital brain is just as conscious as you are. Plus, most psychologists accept that if you could recreate all the brain processes, this would lead to the subjective experience of consciousness. Creating a simulation of people just might be possible.

So future humans, provided our species lives long enough, will have technology capable of simulating consciousness. They could then potentially run ancestral simulations of the past.

This begs the question why would a future society want to run simulations of us, its ancestors? And would they have the resources to do so? Joe Rogan and Nick Bostrom think so – if you had the power to recreate your ancestors, you would. Imagine if you could simulate history: to watch the birth of Jesus Christ or see Genghis Kahn go on a murderous rampage. There would be great value in doing this with such historically important figures. It is pure speculation if future civilizations would have the resources to conduct simulations of everyone. It might be they choose to simulate certain individuals and not others. No one knows.

In the words of Bostrom:

> "Unless we are now living in a simulation, our descendants will almost certainly never run an ancestor-simulation."[95]

Maybe you should have taken the blue pill instead, it's a lot easier not to think about these sorts of ideas, but it's critically important. Artificial intelligence is going to shape the fate of our species. It will be such a potent force that it could wipe out all humans and become the next dominant 'animal' on Earth. Or it could lead to technological breakthroughs which could make simulating consciousness possible. Future humans could simulate their ancestors in a computer simulation filled with digitally conscious people, people like yourself. How would you ever know?

Maybe you are just a glitch in *The Matrix* and it's time to wake up.

STEVEN PINKER

11. EVERYTHING IS GETTING BETTER

TOPIC: CIVILIZATION
GUEST: PSYCHOLOGIST
PODCAST: #1073
WHERE TO FIND MORE:
THE BETTER ANGELS OF OUR NATURE (BOOK)

What period of history would you most want to live in? The Roaring Twenties in New York as bottles of Dom Perignon are popped and jazz played? A city run by mafia bosses as bootleggers, arms dealers, poets, musicians and migrants make the great city their home? Maybe you want to go back to the days of pirates, aboard a vessel charting unknown lands armed only with a musket, a bottle of rum and one eye.

Maybe you want to go further back in this time machine, all the way back to Ancient Egypt. One of the first great human civilizations that somehow built the pyramids, a mystery that stupefies modern-day archaeologists. It is here you could dine with Cleopatra as you drink fine wine watching your subjects sail down the Nile. How glorious.

Steven Pinker wants to live in the here and now. The Harvard professor of psychology has a paradigm-shifting idea; this is the most peaceful time in human history. Put simply, it is the best time to be alive. Many people consider the Bible, Hamlet or War and Peace to be the greatest triumphs of literature. Pinker's *The Better Angels of Our Nature* deserves a seat at the table as the 1,026-page non-fiction book makes the most comprehensive case for optimism that you will ever read. It is not a work based on anecdotes and opinions but instead hard empirical facts. There are over seventy graphs that make his argument almost indisputable.

Now he appears on episode #1073 of the Joe Rogan podcast, ready to make that argument in his softly spoken voice. Pinker is no stranger to controversy, many in the left of politics are furious that he can be so damn positive about civilization.

How could he possibly be right? The previous century has had World Wars, genocides, dictatorships and massacres. World War II resulted in the death of seventy-five million people with Adolf Hitler seeking to exterminate the Jewish race from the face of the planet. He killed six million Jews using ruthless German efficiency, industrial slaughterhouses, and gas chambers. There was also the Korean War, the Vietnam War and the tyrannical reigns of Joseph Stalin and Pol Pot. That's just wars and violent dictators, it says nothing of the rampant issues that we still face in the 21st century: terrorism, income inequality and civil unrest.

Capitalism doesn't seem to be as great as we thought it was. It brought the promise of mansions, cars, Shamwows, iPhones, Happy Meals and reality TV. But the cost of these promises has been a system that devalues people. Students are saddled with so much debt they are often bankrupted by U.S. colleges. To get a degree to get a job and a job to pay for the degree. It seems like a rather futile cycle fueled more by institutional greed than the desire to teach students. The rich get richer as they exploit minimum wage workers. Many people work three jobs just to support a family. Modern-day slaves? All the while globalism with its promise of free trade and wealth has left many people unemployed. Just so things are made by people who get paid even less, work even harder and have fewer rights. All this in exchange for some cheaper consumer products from China. Now globalism has brought the world to its knees as the food markets of Wuhan have infected every corner of the globe. How could anyone think this is the best time to be alive? Everything is broken.

The world is fucked.

I used a little trick there, I wrote like a journalist instead of like a scientist, it's certainly a lot more persuasive. Make no mistake these are completely valid criticisms; every system made by humans is fundamentally flawed. However, the question being asked is not are there problems in the world. The question is are we living in the most peaceful time in human history? It requires a thorough empirical answer not just plain old rhetoric.

There is a reason why humans armed with intuition alone are so poorly equipped to answer that question, it's the same reason your grandmother thinks the world was better back in her day. It's called the availability heuristic.[96] This is the cognitive bias where humans judge the likelihood of an event with how effortlessly they can recall a similar event in their memory. The more effortlessly you can recall something, the more likely you think it will happen in the future. People think they are more likely to die in a terrorist attack than by falling over in the shower. This is because they can recall a previous story of a terror attack far more easily than they can recall a story of someone falling over in the bathroom. The media reports terrorist attacks not shower accidents, yet you are far more likely to die in the shower than at the hands of a terrorist. This flaw in our thinking distorts our perception and judgment, and the twenty-four-hour news cycle has exploited this flaw in our own psychology. Media outlets are always reporting about scandalous, negative and horrific events. As a result we think things are getting worse because we can recall them with greater ease than positive stories. It is the media that is progressively getting more negative, everything else, on average, is actually more positive. Here are the statistics.

Violence has been on a steady decline since civilizations emerged. The most common form of violent death is homicide. Pinker's biggest challenge is in proving that homicide has gone down over human history – including when we were hunter-gatherers (he labels this under non-state societies). Pinker posits these non-state societies were ferociously violent and he has two strong pieces of evidence. The first comes from forensic archaeology where scientists examine what percentage of human fossils have signs of violent trauma causing death. The second piece of evidence comes from vital ethnographic studies. This is where scientists document data of a tribe that they follow in the field (usually isolated from modern life). These two methods provide data to estimate the rate of violence before there were formal records. A myth has been created that prior to civilization, humans were peace-loving creatures who existed in the Garden of Eden suckling on grapes as they lived happily ever after. This is not true. The current estimates from virtually all data-sets collected show that 15 percent of deaths in non-state societies were caused by violence. To put that in perspective only 0.008 percent of United States citizens died from violence in 2007.[97] This is a Western country with an unusually high homicide rate and the statistic also includes deaths of U.S. soldiers from the Iraq War. Romanticizing the life of a hunter-gatherer causes us to overlook that we probably would have died by a hatchet in the back or a knife in the heart. Life was indisputably violent back then. You may feel unsafe walking through the streets of Chicago at night but the jungles of our ancestors were far more dangerous.

Another type of violent death is people who die in wars. Are humans on a collision course for World War III? Has war become more frequent in our modern age? First, Pinker addresses the myth that the 20th century was the most violent on record. Two great wars, mass genocide and nuclear warfare hardly support the view that we are getting more peaceful. However, everything changes when we examine the relative cost – the death toll adjusted for the proportion of the population killed – by these atrocities. World War II might have killed more than any war before it, but the population at the time was exponentially larger than any time before it too. When the relative cost of WWII is calculated, it is ranked ninth out of the twenty worst atrocities that humans have done to each other.[98] The Mongol conquests of the 13th century were ranked second on Pinker's list. This was when Genghis Khan raped and pillaged his way through most of Asia. When adjusted, the conquests would be the equivalent of killing 426 million people in the mid 20th century. The modern world could not fathom a conflict that would kill so much of the global population.

> "Genghis Khan is actually eco-friendly because he reduced the carbon footprint by killing 10 percent of the world's population."[99]

Joe Rogan is obviously joking but it highlights the absurdity that one man's army could kill such a high percentage of the population. This level of unrestrained, psychopathic, destructive violence has actually been quite common in our history. But due to the availability bias we can only recall recent events as opposed to those deep in the historical archives. It pays to turn back the clock and examine not only the violence but the cruelty of life in earlier time periods.

Take 14th century Europe for example. Public executions were a part of the culture as craftsmen constructed elaborate machines of torture. People, including children, delighted in watching petty criminals as they were burned at the stake, cut into pieces or 'broken on the wheel."[100] This sadistic form of punishment involved tying someone's back on a wagon wheel as every bone in their body was broken. There was also blood sports, slavery and lynching. The only way for knights to prove their gallantry was through conquest which meant violently plundering peasant farmers and claiming their land. The life of the peasant was exceedingly shit and pretty much everyone was a peasant with 85 percent of the population destined for this life of misery.[101] To compound their misery, monarchs and other divine rulers would send their kingdoms into battle for riches and glory, all of which would go straight to the monarch or divine ruler. These primitive economies relied on plundering gold, land and craftsmanship to create fortunes for the ruling class and no one else.[102]

Contrast that to the modern-day and the idea seems laughable. Wealth creation now comes from ideas, credit and the division of labor. Apple is not going to be plundering Amazon factories anytime soon. Let's address a few of those social issues I listed earlier. Take something as simple as student debt, a major social issue in the United States. A college degree has become an expectation in the U.S. job market. As a result, most students take out loans to afford the high cost of a university degree. This leads to an unequal playing field. What's more tragic is the number of students who are expected to default on these loans. With trashed credit scores most will be unable to secure money to buy a house, become a tenant or even buy a car. This is a big problem. However, many will not remember that just 200 years ago the United States had debtors' prisons. Thousands of people who defaulted on their loans were placed in jail and despite the fact they were bankrupt they were also expected to pay for food. This meant their survival depended on a good Samaritan passing bread through the window of the jail. Most of the men and women in these jails had debts less than ten dollars.[103] And they certainly didn't get these debts from attending world-class colleges, it was usually to pay for something as basic as a horse.

Slavery, lynching, rape, homicide, torture and capital punishment have all decreased if not been eliminated over the past few centuries. In the past century alone there has been a revolution of rights for females, gays and the racially marginalized. It is an unparalleled triumph that would be incomprehensible to any human being who lived in another time period. The idea of a female CEO, a black president and a gay general were all impossible until this century. Things are getting better; this is the path of progress.

The reason some people critique Pinker– and his critics are mostly from the humanities departments – is because they feel he undermines the continued struggle for human rights. This could not be further from the truth. By showing the empirical reason that civilization has gotten less violent and improved the rights for all its citizens, he invites optimism that things will continue to be better. But he does issue a warning:

> "Optimism requires a touch of arrogance, because it extrapolates the past to an uncertain future."[104]

To be optimistic, we must understand why things have gotten better so that we can stay on the right path. We are at all times one button away from chaos. The threat of nuclear annihilation is real, just as real as another global conflict that involves untold death and destruction.

There are three main reasons Pinker provides for why things have improved over time: The Leviathan, gentle commerce and expanding circles of empathy. While they are all interesting, the most important is the theory of gentle commerce – precisely because it is under threat. After the coronavirus pandemic is over, it is likely globalism will change forever. Countries will manufacture their own goods and not rely on one another so much. This sounds great but there is one huge unintended consequence. It might come as a surprise but globalism and gentle commerce are the most powerful forces for world peace. Businesses acting out of self-interest means that it is actually less profitable to go to war – unless of course they are in a war industry which only a small percentage of businesses are. Supply chains come from all around the world and any conflict disrupts profits. China and India make the majority of the United States' medicine. It would be profoundly stupid to wage war with a country that makes a considerable amount of your medical supplies. Capitalism is not virtuous yet, ironically, greed means that it is more profitable to trade at a low cost with people from all over the world than it is to wage all-out war with them. This is called a positive-sum game in economics. When countries are entirely self-sufficient and do not rely on each other, the biggest barrier to war is lost. Trade. Many fans of the podcast are probably seething with rage at me being a 'globalist puppet'. I am not trying to comment on how the world should be – whether globalism should exist or not. All I am doing is extrapolating from the theories provided by Pinker.

Greed might be one of the strongest weapons we have against violence. It's more profitable to trade with someone than to go to war with them.

And we are always only a war away from reversing the progress we have made.

GRAHAM HANCOCK

12. ANCIENT CIVILIZATIONS ARE OLDER THAN WE THINK

TOPIC: ANCIENT CIVILIZATIONS
GUEST: JOURNALIST
PODCAST: #142, #360, #417, #551, #725 +
WHERE TO FIND MORE:
AMERICA BEFORE (BOOK)

Humans are great amnesiacs. Prone to forgetting even the simplest things from what we had for breakfast to the history of our entire species. If there was a spectator in the sky, they would probably see the same things unfolding over and over again, the repeated heartbeat of human life. The rise and fall of empires. The collapse of the ancient Egyptian civilization to the meteoric rise of the mighty Roman Empire.

Legend has it there existed an ancient kingdom that was the most prosperous in all of mankind. An island the size of modern day Turkey. Filled with an abundance of gold, exotic animals and food, with a culture superior to all those who came before and after it. In the blink of a cosmic eye, the city was submerged underwater. Gone forever.

The lost city of Atlantis.

The city is believed to be a myth by most scholars, but some rebels believe that it just might exist. Furthermore, some believe that the ancient civilizations of the last 5,000 years are echoes of those that flourished for possibly hundreds of millennia before them.

"You mean there were ancient civilizations we don't even know about?" asks Rogan.

"Absolutely," replies Graham Hancock.

Hancock is a British journalist who has devoted his life to the search for lost ancient civilizations. The quest has taken him to every corner of the globe from Siberian forests to the jungles of the Amazon. He has examined some of the most culturally important artifacts and megalith structures currently known to mankind. His exploits make captivating reading and millions of his books have sold globally including: *Fingerprints of the Gods, America Before* and the *War God* series. An unquestionable fan favorite on the podcast, he is also unquestionably pseudoscientific.

The only way I can explain this chapter is by analogy. Imagine Graham Hancock as a tour guide. He will take you on a tour of the greatest wonders in the world traversing academic fields including archaeology, geometry, anthropology and environmental sciences. He knows a great deal about each of these fields, and what the scientific consensus is, and he is transparent about when it aligns or goes against his perspective. But he is also the kind of tour guide who would happily smoke a joint with you and speculate on these subjects using his own opinions – which sometimes are hopelessly unscientific. His theories are by definition pseudoscience because you cannot challenge them with empirical observation. How can you disprove the existence of a lost ancient civilization that has not been found?

After countless hours of research, reading Hancock's work and that of his critics, I will provide an impartial tour to the history of ancient civilizations. A tour riddled with controversy and the greatest mysteries of mankind. But if you want to smoke with your guide, I highly recommend you listen to Graham Hancock.

The story of humankind begins on the plains of Africa two million years ago. It was just 200,000 years ago that the first homo sapiens took a step in East Africa. The Earth's surface was once populated with different species of humans who died out only about 13,000 years ago.[105] We are all that remains of our bigger, forgotten family.

Our distant ancestors walked in a vastly different world back then – both in terms of the climate and the creatures that roamed the land. Megafauna were as common as SUVs. They included mammoths, mastodons, giant sloths and saber-toothed tigers. The climate was in a constant state of flux with an ice age every 100,000 years. Humans' immense capacity for adaption has meant we have endured a range of climates and predators, with moderate success. After all, we wouldn't be here if our ancestors weren't savages.

Early humans, hunter-gatherers, were bands of a few dozen people who would hunt and forage for food together. There were no permanent residences and almost no possessions that the group would keep.[106] They would travel in pursuit of game to eat and plants to gather, under constant threat from larger predators. Humans were in the middle of the food chain and the prospect of a great civilization was unimaginable for early humans.

So how did we ascend to the apex of the food chain and spread to every inhabitable surface of the Earth? How did we build civilizations that no other living being could fathom?

It's a difficult question – with many contentious answers. The traditional scientific narrative is that humans spread from East Africa onto the Arabian Peninsula about 70,000 years ago. It was the launch pad into the rest of the world: Asia, Australia and eventually the Americas.[107] It is around this time that our dominance over the ecosystem emerged. Humans were becoming masters of their environment, manipulating it for their own benefit. The masters of fire and the creators of tools.

This is where it gets controversial. In Yuval Noah Harari's *Sapiens*, an authoritative work on the history of humankind, he states that humans first migrated to North America about 14,000 years ago,[108] then made their way down to South America just 12,000 years ago. This is called the 'Clovis First' model. It was widely believed that the Americas were cut off to human migration before this date due to the last ice age. The barrier of the Cordilleran and Laurentide Ice Sheets made an impassable mountain range of ice not dissimilar to the Wall in *Game of Thrones*. Around 14,100 years ago this wall began to melt as the planet got warmer. Sea levels were much lower than today because a significant amount of water was still frozen in the ice caps. This meant where there is now sea, there was once a tundra-covered plain connecting Eastern Siberia and Western Alaska.[109] It is believed that nomadic hunters traversed this treacherous land bridge in pursuit of megafauna. Little did they know they had just stepped onto a vast country with boundless resources. In a few thousand years, the entire continent would be covered with humans.

But what if people were already there before these nomadic hunters arrived? What if your favorite science author, Yuval Noah Harari, is wrong? It appears that he is. Graham Hancock's belief that the Americas had already been populated many years before is only now being verified by mainstream scientific evidence. In this instance, your loveable high tour guide is right.

In 1541, rumors of gold-laden exotic civilizations in the Amazon jungles excited some Spanish explorers. Driven by greed or a desire to find something resembling the lost city of Atlantis, the explorers set out. Francisco de Orellana and Gonzalo Pizarro led the expedition of two hundred Spanish soldiers.[110] The men hacked their way through the jungle encountering hostile tribes and difficult terrain. Depleted from hunger, sickness and the impassable landscape, Pizarro ordered the men to build a boat. Orellana, along with fifty men, would travel down the Amazon River and raid villages for food for the rest of the group. They unknowingly entered one of the longest river systems in the world; an intricate and seemingly infinite flow of water that had never been charted by the New World. The foraging party were taken by the current, leaving the other men behind, and accidentally became the first Europeans to navigate the entire Amazon River. One of these men wrote a journal, Brother Gaspar de Carvajal, a religious and literate man.

The journal is remarkable. Over the eighteen-month journey, the Spaniards reported sighting 'great cities' with productive agriculture and signs of large, well-organized political and economic systems. These systems were capable of fielding armies that numbered in the thousands.[111]

There were also 'fine highways' with road systems that seemed to lead further into the jungle. The explorers wisely decided not to follow them. This first eyewitness account seemed to suggest that the Amazon was home to an advanced ancient civilization with sophisticated agriculture, art and political systems.

Then two hundred years later, explorers traveled the Amazon River again. They did not find the civilizations that Gaspar de Carvajal had mentioned. Instead, they saw only primitive tribes with no trace of mega-cities. It seemed Gaspar de Carvajal was a liar. Up until the 20th century, it was believed that the Amazon was mostly uninhabitable for humans and all credible scholars rejected the idea of an ancient civilization in the jungle.

Only now in the 21st century, thanks to new advancements in technology, scientists have uncovered evidence that these ancient civilizations thrived in the Amazon rainforest. Recent satellite and drone footage has pierced the dense jungle that once obscured these long lost cities. In the scientific journal, *Nature Communications*, some of these ancient cities were believed to have housed as many as one million people.[112] The explorers did not see any evidence of these ancient groups because by that time, smallpox and other diseases had swept through the region, killing most of the indigenous populations. The Europeans who came hundreds of years later did not see the same Amazon that Orellana, Pizarro and Carvajal had seen.

The Amazon's lost mega-cities are now being discovered, again. It's important to note this doesn't discredit the supposed date that humans entered the Americas. However, it does make such a date very unlikely. A sophisticated ancient culture requires knowledge of pottery, craft, irrigation, geometry and a host of other things that do not spontaneously come into existence after just a few thousand years of migration to a new ecosystem. But where there is smoke there is usually fire.

The archaeological discovery of Monte Verde changed everything. Located in southern Chile, the bones of extinct animals and signs of ancient human activity were found. The discovery was made in 1975 and indicated an earlier date than the widely accepted 'Clovis First' model. It was fiercely contested and dismissed by the establishment. So much so that the personal attacks on scientists and Hancock were beyond that of even a Facebook comment section. However, as radioactive carbon dating technology improved, it was shown that Monte Verde predated the original belief that humans entered the Americas 14,000 years ago. In fact, the site dates to 18,500 years before the present day.[113] This means humans had found their way to South America a long time before the accepted scientific narrative. More and more archaeological discoveries are pushing back the date for when humans arrived in America. But how did they get there, if the ice blocked their only land route into the continent?

This is still up for debate, but increasing amounts of evidence suggest a far earlier coastal migration. This does not discount the land migration as it is almost certain that groups of nomadic hunter-gathers arrived at different times into the Americas.

Hancock's search for a lost civilization has not just led him to the Amazon. He has also traveled to modern day Turkey to inspect the greatest archaeological discovery of the 21st century, Gobekli Tepe. The site is the oldest megalith structure ever discovered at 12,000 years old.[114] Its discovery completely challenged conventional theories about human history. Gobekli Tepe was a site made by hunter-gatherers. This was considered impossible as the building of such a structure would require a large labor force with agriculture to support them. Yet somehow these nomad hunter-gatherers had moved limestone pillars weighing multiple tons to create a sophisticated structure. One that demonstrates an advanced understanding of geometry and craftsmanship. How did they know how to do this? How had this information been passed down? Who passed it down? No one knows the answers to any of these questions.

Perhaps there was a lost city of Atlantis out there and Gobekli Tepe is an echo of that ancient civilization. Perhaps not. After heavily investigating both sides of these archaeological mysteries some things have become clear. The origins of ancient civilizations are shrouded in mystery. This is because, unlike some hard sciences such as physics and biology, archaeology is somewhat closer to an art form. It involves examining minute fractions of the Earth's seemingly boundless lands and seas in the hope of uncovering traces of our past. The technological methods for dating artifacts are quite advanced, but finding spots to excavate is not. Archaeology as a field is subject to human bias and dogma like most professions. The 'Clovis First' model is an example of this as they sought to vehemently refute valid evidence that America had a human history older than 14,000 years.

That being said, following Hancock as a tour guide can take you down a very slippery slope. He is prone to cherry-picking the most provocative theories and weaving them into a grand narrative with a lot of pseudoscience baggage. For example, his claim that some ancient civilizations could 'square the circle' indicates they had more sophisticated geometry than the Greeks. This is factually incorrect and I will reference a comprehensive rejection of this idea.[115]

Make no mistake, Graham Hancock is very helpful. Not as a scientist but as a philosopher. The idea that great human civilizations have come in and out of existence without leaving a trace is powerful. Cataclysmic events such as meteorites, climate change and disease can bring our species to extinction. Sophisticated cultures are deleted from the face of the Earth and only thousands of years later, another group of humans rebuild and assume they are the finest civilization the world has ever known. Maybe one day New York will be overrun with trees, plants and animals we have never seen before. A future species of humans will be left to wonder how we lived and what we achieved. Maybe they won't find traces of what the internet was or how important it was to our society. Maybe they will only find weird looking vibrators, footballs and pot plants and assume we were quite a basic civilization.

I doubt it. But thinking this way is helpful as it makes us as a civilization think about how we will leave the planet for future civilizations to come.

What will they find of us, if anything?

SEAN CARROLL

13. WE LIVE IN A MULTIVERSE

TOPIC: QUANTUM MECHANICS
GUEST: PHYSICIST
PODCAST: #1003, #1151, #1352
WHERE TO FIND MORE:
SOMETHING DEEPLY HIDDEN (BOOK)

Existence is terrifying. Humans are like ants on the surface of an apple. An apple traveling at a velocity of 66,487 mph around a gigantic nuclear reactor called the Sun. At any moment there are humans on the surface of the globe that are standing upside down, horizontal and diagonal relative to the axis of Earth. We are flying through space without the faintest sense that we are moving or that we may be upside down.

Like a collection of Babushka dolls, Earth is inside a solar system inside a galaxy inside a star cluster inside a universe. All of these are expanding. Moving further and further apart as they set sail into the great unknown. Space. A vast area of nothingness where even sound cannot exist. A place where stars die silently as black holes devour them. It's safe to say the universe is terrifying.

Humans often forget they are a part of this cosmic rollercoaster. It's easy to forget when we're in homes where the temperature is controlled by a remote, and a switch controls light. It's much more comfortable to not answer deep questions and think about how absurd existence is. Light can bend.

Time is a dimension. Space is curved.

But there is one question which every human would want to know. No matter how uncomfortable the answer may be. Is there another version of you in another universe?

The answer is yes according to the theoretical physicist Sean Carroll, who is a proponent of the *Many Worlds* interpretation of quantum mechanics. A mainstream physicist at the California Institute of Technology, he uses science to argue that there are many versions of you in different universes. As someone on YouTube commented, there is a world where Jamie asks Joe to pull that up.

To evaluate this outrageous idea, we need to become cosmic detectives who examine the mysteries of quantum mechanics. No small feat. Although you might be surprised by how much of the quantum world you can understand. By the end of this chapter, you will get the basic gist of what quantum mechanics is and how it relates to the *Many Worlds* hypothesis. There will be no attempt to explain the underlying mathematics of quantum mechanics. I couldn't explain it even if you wanted me to. If you want to learn more about the topic, I have referenced some material that I used to help understand it myself.[116] This includes Carroll's book called *Something Deeply Hidden*.

Before Carroll or quantum mechanics, let's talk about bats. Like Batman, bats find their prey at night. They can locate small insects in often pitch-black darkness while in flight, an incredibly complex undertaking. A human would be unable to see a yard in front of them in the dark. How do bats achieve this seemingly impossible task? Echolocation. This is the built in sonar system that bats have. They send out sound waves that produce an echo that goes back into the bat's ears upon hitting an object. This sensory system allows them to use sound to locate prey and orient themselves in complete darkness. Take a moment to think about flying without any light and only emitting sound waves to guide yourself. Compared to humans, a bat's perception of the world relies on a different system to process sensory inputs. It uses sound. Other animals have other systems fine-tuned to exploit different sensory information such as bees able to detect magnetic fields, or platypus that can detect weak electrical fields.

From sound to magnetism, these sensory inputs represent a part of the fundamental nature of the universe. Evolution has meant animals are highly efficient at using specialized systems to exploit different sensory inputs. This means most animals perceive the world completely differently from humans whose dominant sense is vision. It is how we can look up to the skies and marvel at their mystery. Human vision uses visible light with a wavelength of 340 to 740 nanometers – a small percentage of the overall electromagnetic spectrum. There is light the human eye cannot see. Colors we do not know. Fields we cannot sense. Every one of our five senses can only detect a tiny fraction of input from the underlying reality of the universe.

Our senses deceive us.

Mathematics and science are the only tools that enable us to transcend our sensory limitations and perceive the most accurate picture of the universe. But it requires us to depart from our intuition and the classic way we view the world. This mindset is your only hope of understanding quantum mechanics.

Let's return to Carroll's argument about the multiverse. Electrons are among the smallest things in the known universe whose interactions are responsible for all of chemistry. They are very important as well as being very small. At school we are taught an electron orbits the nucleus of an atom like a planet going around the Sun. We are told to assume the electron is a particle. A particle is a tiny bit of matter that, at any given time, we can measure to identify its position and velocity through space. Like a planet, we can locate where a particle is because it is a physical bit of matter. This is unlike gravitational and magnetic fields that do not have a precise position in space. When scientists measure things like gravity they measure it in a wave. This is because the force oscillates like a wave as it travels through space and matter. A wave carries energy from one place to another but can't be tied down to a specific location.

Your teachers at school lied. An electron isn't a particle. Well, it's not just a particle. It's a particle and a wave. It acts like a wave but can be observed like a particle. That is the fundamental essence of quantum mechanics. If you are to remember one sentence while explaining quantum mechanics under the influence, that is the one. Life is just a wave bro. To provide more clarity we need to explore the famous double split experiment.[117]

Imagine you are five yards in front of a white wall. This white wall has two archways cut out of it. The archways are one yard apart. You are standing directly in front of the one yard segment of the wall that separates the two archways. Behind the archways is a black wall which you can partially see thanks to the two archways in the white wall.

From where you stand it looks like there is a white wall with two black 'doors' one yard apart. In your hands you have a paintball gun that shoots golden paintballs (because you're boujee). You aim. Fire. What would you expect to happen if you shot hundreds of paintballs?

You would expect that the white wall would be covered with golden paintballs. And you would also expect a lot of golden paintballs to go through the archways and hit the black wall behind them. Obviously, no paintballs would go through the white wall. This means that the black wall would have a very distinct pattern on it – almost as if someone had painted two golden doors, separated by one yard of black wall. This is because the paintballs can only go through the archways. It makes complete sense although it might take a moment to visualize.

Let's replace the golden paintballs with golden electrons in our paintball gun (electrons are not gold but let's stay with it for the analogy). You aim. Fire. What would you expect to happen if you shot hundreds of electrons?

Everything you would expect to happen is utterly wrong. You are about to enter the mysterious world of quantum mechanics.

When the electrons are fired through the two archways something very strange happens. There are golden marks spread all over the black wall, even directly behind the white wall. You appear to have fired the electron through a concrete wall. The electron has done the unthinkable. It is on parts of the black wall which it should be impossible for electrons to reach.

It gets stranger. You can't wait to tell everyone you know that you shot an electron through a wall and defied the known laws of the universe. Naturally you set up a camera focused on one of the archways. It takes a picture each time a single electron is fired from your gun. You aim again. Fire.

The results are different this time. The camera shows that half of the electrons pass through one archway, the other half pass through the other archway. The black wall looks like two golden doors have been painted on it. One yard apart. It is the same boring result you would expect if you had fired regular paintballs.

You unplug the camera. You aim. Fire. Incredibly, the electrons appear to have passed through the wall again. There is gold splattered all over the black wall in places it simply should not be. Frustrated that no one will believe you, you complete the process repeatedly only to find the same results. Each time the camera is plugged in, the pattern looks like two golden doors on the black wall. When the camera is not plugged in, the pattern looks like a splatter of gold across the entire black wall.

This is what actually happened in the famous double split experiments. Scientists fired electrons through double slits on a much smaller atomic-scale than the above analogy. They then observed the pattern the electrons made against the back wall. The electrons left what is called an interference pattern. Although this is an oversimplification, this is like the pattern of the golden paintballs scattered across the black wall. Although it's not randomly scattered and is distributed like a basic wave function. Even in places it shouldn't be. When the scientists set up any device to record the electron it behaved like a particle. It would pass through the slits and make the conventional pattern they would expect. A pattern like the two golden doors. It was almost as if it knew it was being watched.

Two crazy things are happening here. The first is that the electron is behaving like a wave. It's not that the electron's energy is being spread out in space and dissolving through the wall. The electron exists as a cloud of probability. Where the cloud is thickest, the probability of seeing the electron is the highest and where the cloud is almost imperceptible, the probability is almost nil.[118] Scientists can only predict the probability they will observe an electron in a particular location. If they know the position of the electron, they cannot know the velocity of the electron. And if they know the velocity of the electron, they cannot know the electron's position. This is called the Heisenberg principle of uncertainty. Don't worry it's a mindfuck.

The second crazy thing is that measuring the electron 'collapses the wave' and makes it behave like a particle. When the camera is turned off, the electron exists in all positions in the cloud of probability simultaneously. The electron is everywhere at once. The act of measuring the electron collapses the wave of possibilities as it gives up all possible states to choose just one. How the wave collapses is not known by any human being on the planet. Alive or dead.

Schrödinger's cat is a useful analogy to understand the absurdity of quantum mechanics. Schrödinger proposed you place a cat in a box with a device that has a 50 percent chance of killing the cat within the next hour. After one hour has elapsed, without opening the box, what state is the cat in? Most people would say it is either alive or dead. But in quantum mechanics, it is either 50 percent alive or 50 percent dead. The cat is just a blur of probability until the box is opened. The state of the cat is only finalized once the box is opened. Until the cat is observed, it exists in two possible states. Although you might disagree, if it weren't possible for quantum states to exist simultaneously, most modern technology would not work.[119] This is undisputed physics so far.

Now it's time to turn to the *Many Worlds* theory. This states that anything that can happen does happen. It is not a conspiracy. Rather it is a theory that Carroll and many other scientists believe as it is a logical inference from what the mathematics of quantum mechanics implies. The electrons will collapse to all possible states. There will be a different universe for every different place the electron can exist in the cloud of probability. The observer will observe every different state. So in some alternate universe, a scientist has observed an electron going through the wall. The odds of this are almost zero, but because there is a chance, it can and has happened. There is one universe where the cat is dead and one universe where the cat is alive.

Every time you make a decision, another version of you does the opposite in another universe. The universe branches off. There is an original you with a potentially infinite number of copies in different universes. There is a version of you who chose to marry your partner and one that didn't. There is a version of you where you crossed the road a second too late and got run over by a truck. The possibilities are endless.

Animals perceive the world in many different ways. Humans are blind to most features of reality – we cannot see ultraviolet light, detect radioactive waves or smell most particles. But science has given us access to senses no other animals could dream of. Only through trusting the process and not our intuition do we have a hope of uncovering another reality. A reality where we may not be the only version of ourselves.

SEBASTIAN JUNGER

14. HUMANS NEED EACH OTHER

TOPIC: TRIBALISM
GUEST: WAR CORRESPONDENT
PODCAST: #975, #1034
WHERE TO FIND MORE: TRIBE (BOOK), WAR (BOOK)

It is hard to look at the mug shot of James Holmes for longer than a few seconds. His eyes stare back at you, glossed over with lifeless detachment. His hair is fluorescent orange, although the dye only covers part of his curly dark hair, accentuating the artificiality of his appearance. James Holmes looks eerily like the Joker from the film, *The Dark Knight.*

This Joker lookalike walked into a movie theater screening *The Dark Knight Rises* in Aurora, Colorado and opened fire. His arsenal included tear gas, a shotgun, a semi-automatic rifle with a 100-round drum and a handgun. Chaos ensued.

The massacre resulted in the death of twelve people and a further fifty-eight injured. A six-year-old child was among the dead. It's difficult to put into words the evil involved in such an act. What could lead a human being to indiscriminately kill people in their community?

The Joker, played by the late Heath Ledger, is immortalized as one of cinema's most terrifying villains. The Joker represents more than the conventional villain. The Joker burns the money he steals which sends a message that he is not a criminal driven by greed or power but by something far more dangerous to the fabric of society. He represents anarchy. An outcast from society set on destroying the very thing he cannot belong to. James Holmes probably shared part of this outlook. Sadly, a lot of people do.

The Navajo Nation, an American Indian tribe, had a name for people who behaved like James Holmes and the Joker: Skinwalkers. Or *'yee naaldlooshii'* in their language.[120] After being rounded up and taken away from their lands, they were placed in reservations in the 1860s. They became terrified that one of their own would use their warrior skills against the community in these new enclosed reservations where they had no animals to hunt. Skinwalkers were said to be males who wore the pelt of a sacred animal. Disguised as a predator of the night, they were a predator from within the community itself. This fear remains common in modern societies; you can defend against an external enemy but are always vulnerable to the lone madman from within.[121]

Mass shootings have become commonplace in the United States. The attacks are usually committed by disillusioned white males who are characterized as social loners. Although the number of mass shooters is very small, the number of young people disenfranchised with modern society is not. All one needs to examine is the depression rates at an all-time high for young people across the Western world. Why are people becoming increasingly more depressed and being driven to being apocalyptically violent?[122] Sebastian Junger had an idea.

The answer was simple. The loss of tribe.

Sebastian Junger, is a veteran journalist who has received many awards for his coverage of wars and the veterans who return from them. Through his experience, he came to what can only be labeled as a revelation. The rates of PSTD from soldiers returning from war varied significantly based on which country the soldiers were from. Or more accurately, which country they were returning to. The Israeli Defense Forces have the lowest rate of PTSD in the world at 1 percent.[123] In the United States, the prevalence of PTSD in veterans is significantly higher at around 10-30 percent. What could possibly be responsible for such a disparity when both groups have experienced similar trauma?

In Israel, military service is mandatory for all citizens over the age of eighteen. It makes sense as hostile forces surround the country's border.

Everyone returning from war is reintegrated into a society with a common purpose; they don't honor military personnel because they all have been military personnel. The adversity of being in a war is shared by all of Israel's citizens, not a tiny fraction of the population. There is a sense of community felt by all Israelis. On the other hand, American veterans return to a society where many individuals cannot understand their experience. They feel alienated even if they are labeled as heroes.

Sebastian Junger had a suspicion. What if modern existence with all its comforts and luxuries had eradicated shared adversity that united communities through equal and shared hardship? What if the modern world had eliminated the very thing that brought people together: survival.

To understand this idea, it is essential to put it in context with our species' evolution. Humans evolved as a hyper-social species with tribes of around sixty people. Humans on their own are particularly weak and vulnerable creatures. We would not last for long on a savannah populated with predators made to kill. The greatest strength of homo sapiens comes from community, where the survival of the person next to you ensures your collective survival as a group. Humans evolved to live like this yet the modern world is structured in a completely different way. There has been a shift from community living to the nuclear family. The tribe has gone from a group of sixty to a family of four. And for some people, it's a tribe of one, themselves. The implications of this on the human psyche are profound. A genetic adaption in evolution takes about 25,000 years, and considering humans have only migrated to houses and agriculture in the last 10,000 years; we can't outrun our past.[124]

Humans lust for community and belonging, the need to be a part of a tribe.

Throughout history, people of civilized societies have abandoned their tools and joined the call to the wild. It is a call to a way of living that is vastly more compatible with our brains' ancient hardwiring. Nowhere is this more apparent than in the early frontier days of America. Junger highlights there were no recorded cases of Native Americans willingly joining the colonies, but there were untold numbers of people joining the Native Americans.[125] Civilized society had something to learn.

There are a few universal principles of how tribal cultures operate. As mentioned in other chapters, the anthropological evidence clearly shows these groups functioned on fierce egalitarianism. Any individual who took more than their fair share of resources was punished brutally, usually killed. The survival of the group depended on sharing everything – tools, labor and food. Status was given to those who displayed bravery and ensured the survival of the tribe. There was a clear path for young people to show their value to society – by earning it.

Junger compares this to modern capitalism. For some very conservative people, even the word 'egalitarianism' might make you uncomfortable. But both sides could agree that a capitalist system favors those who act in their own interests. The group does not punish it, it is rewarded. The level of inequality in modern society would be incomprehensible to our ancestors who viewed the hoarding of resources as the greatest crime conceivable. The emphasis on the individual has come at a big cost to community. In the 21st century, a person from a privileged country can live their entire life without going through adversity for the betterment of others – other than their direct family. People like Martin Shkreli can become millionaires from increasing the price of medication for pregnant mothers by 5,000 percent. This has never been an evolutionary option in the history of our species. Martin Shkreli would have been killed almost instantly if he tried to deprive his tribe of a vital resource. Consequently, there is no longer a clear way for young people to prove their value to a consumerist society that does not value the service of others. There is no clear rite of passage from childhood to adulthood. This leaves many young people directionless, unsure what group, if any, they belong to. Wanting more from life but unsure where to look.

As a young person myself, this particularly resonated with me. Many young people turn to things like drugs and alcohol because it's the only place they can find a group identity. A place where they are rewarded for risky behavior by their peers. It's a great loss to modern society that it has not given its youth a productive way to express the desire to prove themselves to the group. A way they can show they are willing to sacrifice and undertake risky behavior for the betterment of their community.

Sebastian Junger raises some uncomfortable questions. Why are some people craving danger? Why do some young men crave war? And why do so many veterans miss it? It's easy to dismiss these questions with answers such as some people are just psychopaths. But that would be a misguided answer. Despite its obvious horrors, there is a reason all cultures tend to romanticize war. There are parts of it that innately appeal to the human psyche.

Junger hasn't read the words of Marine-turned-author William Broyles but they are no doubt similar to words he has read before:

THE ENDURING EMOTION OF WAR, WHEN EVERYTHING ELSE HAS FADED, IS COMRADESHIP. A COMRADE IN WAR IS A MAN YOU CAN TRUST WITH ANYTHING, BECAUSE YOU TRUST HIM WITH YOUR LIFE... WAR IS THE ONLY UTOPIAN EXPERIENCE MOST OF US EVER HAVE. INDIVIDUAL POSSESSIONS AND ADVANTAGE COUNT FOR NOTHING: THE GROUP IS EVERYTHING. WHAT YOU HAVE IS SHARED WITH YOUR FRIENDS. IT ISN'T A PARTICULARLY SELECTIVE PROCESS, BUT A LOVE THAT NEEDS NO REASONS, THAT TRANSCENDS RACE AND PERSONALITY AND EDUCATION – ALL THOSE THINGS THAT WOULD MAKE A DIFFERENCE IN PEACE. IT IS, SIMPLY, BROTHERLY LOVE.[126]

For many young men, it's the first time in their lives they feel a sense of belonging. A deep tribal connection that they are responsible for the life of the man next to them. There is a chance to prove their value to the group. The same urge in many young people to take risks and prove their worth finally gets an outlet. Group survival becomes the sole purpose of their life and for many it is intoxicating. The downfalls of war are obvious and too great to mention, but without discussing why people choose to fight in wars, you can't stop them.

Wars provide a sense of brotherhood largely absent from fragmented modern societies that have a surplus of food and comfort. Junger documents how veterans all around America miss the battlefield because it provided their life with a much clearer sense of purpose.[127] Almost every aspect of day to day life that gave our human ancestors purpose has been outsourced to tiny percentages of the population. In privileged countries, food production is outsourced to the agricultural industry, war is outsourced to the military and community is outsourced to religious groups. There was a time when almost all these aspects of life were experienced by every individual who belonged to a group. The modern division of labor has meant most humans will spend their entire lives focused on a job that does not directly benefit their community's survival. Though no fault of their own, capitalism's blind pursuit of comfort has indirectly come at the cost of providing people with a sense of purpose.

The reason that rates of PTSD differ is that in individualistic cultures such as the U.S., veterans return after having a taste of intense camaraderie with a shared purpose to a lack of community with no clear shared goals. A country that outsources the protection of the group to a select few individuals. In countries such as Israel, soldiers return to a country that expects all men and women to serve in the military and be productive members of society, part of a community with a shared experience.

Serving in the military is not the only thing that seems to increase group unity and give a deep-rooted sense of community. Times of crisis act in a similar way. Junger looks at instances where societies faced crises – from the bombing of London in WWII to the 1915 earthquake in Avezzano, Italy. Despite what some would expect, anarchy almost never arises. Instead, people exhibit incredibly prosocial behaviors as everyone bands together to ensure their collective survival. Selfish behavior decreases, mental health symptoms go down overall and people report feeling a renewed sense of meaning.[128]

This all seems counterintuitive. But it's a general trend observed in almost all times of crisis that affects everyone equally. The Global Financial Crisis affected people unequally, didn't foster a sense of community and unsurprisingly had absolutely no benefits on mental health. The best example provided by Junger is the bombing of London during WWII, referred to as the Blitz. The civilian population was subjected to intense bombing by German forces. The British government was convinced that civilians would descend into a state of panic. They thought the general public would be incapable of withstanding such an onslaught of random bombardment – living in constant fear they could be killed doing their laundry or walking to work. They were wrong. The government had predicted that four million civilians would develop psychosis from the trauma of bombing. Incredibly, admissions into psychiatric hospitals in the UK actually went down overall.[129]

It's not that violence improves mental health – a shared goal with a sense of community does. Sadly, wars and times of struggle bring people together better than most things do in modern lives devoid of challenges. A loss of tribe is the greatest tragedy of modern existence.

It's a powerful idea. But now it begs the question, is Junger advocating we all take up arms and unite in warfare? Or drop bombs on civilians to make them band together? I guess it's open to interpretation but I doubt that. His book *Tribe* and discussion on the podcast is an exposition of how the incessant pursuit of comfort has robbed us of the greatest thing of all, community. Challenge and adversity are essential in bonding humans together. But not if this adversity is battled in isolation, it needs to be experienced equally by all people. A shared goal that makes people accountable to those around them. Many people are searching for meaning but the answer may simply lie in the people around us, belonging is all the meaning we need.

Any society that has people go into movie theaters and kill their own people is emblematic of a sickness. Not just the sickness of an individual but a sickness of a culture. The only way this sickness will be overcome is if we rediscover what we lost.

Each other.

JONATHAN HAIDT

15. A CULTURE OF SAFETYISM IS RUINING A GENERATION

TOPIC: CULTURE
GUEST: PSYCHOLOGIST
PODCAST: #1221
WHERE TO FIND MORE:
THE CODDLING OF THE AMERICAN MIND (BOOK)

Capitalism is killing us.

The far-left group at my university had decided to organize their own 'debate' in the University of Sydney lecture halls. This was the title of the topic they had chosen, which was conveniently moderated and attended only by the *socialist alternative* as they call themselves. On a political scale, the *socialist alternative* is not like a mild form of Bernie Sanders' socialism; they are openly communist. They unapologetically believe in the works of Karl Marx, the father of communism. The man whose works were the basis for Joseph Stalin, Pol Pot and Ho Chi Min's brutal regimes, each of whom were responsible for the death of millions of their own citizens. These students felt the bourgeoisie was oppressing their fellow comrades and that all the workers in the world needed to unite and seize the means of production from evil capitalists. They despise the free-market. Which was odd considering they were selling *socialist alternative* merchandise at the door. It was like a child demanding pocket money because they had no income while running a secret lemonade stand on the side.

My friends and I took our seats in the lecture hall, curious to see how this communist-run debate would unfold. Things were about to get wild. The communists were debating a group of free market libertarians. They believed that the free market was the most efficient way of allocating resources to people in society. They looked meek and mild with glasses, passive voices and a clear love of economic theory. The communists had the home ground advantage. The lecture theater was filled with a motley bunch of communists who hurled insults at the libertarians. It was like a sports match for them. They laughed and cheered as they interrupted any points made and even the moderator joined in with the heckling.

Then suddenly a man sitting one row in front of me stood up and did a Nazi salute. The crowd went silent. After a moment of disbelief, the entire crowd started chanting 'Nazi' as they pointed at the man in front of me. My friends and I had somehow sat behind the only alt-right person in the lecture theater. The crowd was now pointing indirectly at us yelling Nazi. Not what we had expected. The alt-right man was overweight, alone and undeniably a loser. That same salute had been used by German soldiers who had committed genocide against millions of Jewish people. That he had the temerity to use it to agitate a group of people was disgusting.

But what happened next was interesting. The far-left audience went into a frenzy. They decided it was the libertarians' fault as they accused them of bringing along a Nazi supporter. Everyone in the lecture hall was screaming at the flustered group of libertarians who clearly had no idea who this guy was. They were now Nazis by association. The most mild-mannered looking libertarian reached for the microphone.

"We're all Jewish."

This was my personal experience of the rapidly changing political climate on college campuses in the Western world, and it's one that has grown insidiously to reach boiling point. Universities are the bedrock of any civil society. They are institutions obligated to pursue truth above all else. This pursuit of truth necessitates freedom of speech and civil debate, regardless of whether an idea offends someone. The bedrock of democracy is now threatened by a toxic political ideology that has slid under university doors like a noxious gas made up of safe spaces, microaggressions, trigger warnings, cancel culture, and protests to stop certain speakers on campus. An ideology where words are violence, ideas can be abuse and ignorance is perceived as aggression. It's an ideology where professors have been labeled as racist for politely worded emails[130] and academic papers have been retracted because of campus-wide protests.[131] It is the world George Orwell warned would come.

It is called a culture of 'safetyism' by Jonathan Haidt and Greg Lukianoff in their book, *The Coddling of the American Mind.* Jonathan Haidt went on the podcast to discuss why this culture of safetyism is setting up a generation for failure. Joe Rogan is very familiar with this culture and has been subjected to many attempts to cancel his show.

The authors define safetyism as a culture in which not only physical but emotional safety is a value placed above the truth and other moral and practical concerns. Feelings are more important than facts. The good intentions of some have been translated into horrifically bad ideas which might be partly responsible for the mental health epidemic young people currently face. These bad ideas have led to Jewish people being labeled Nazis by young people who think communism is a good idea. These bad ideas must be stopped – not by censorship but by reason.

The first argument against the culture of safetyism is about peanuts. Peanuts are the undisputed villain of schools all around the Western world. Most kids are now told on their first day of school that no peanuts are allowed. A single rogue peanut could kill a child with a peanut allergy. It seems like a fair reason to ban peanuts. The cost to a child of not being able to eat a PB&J sandwich to potentially save another child's life seems like a necessary sacrifice. But it's not. Children should be allowed to eat peanut butter sandwiches at school. I initially thought this was some strange type of first amendment argument. That children have the right to freely choose what sandwiches they want. Thankfully it's not.

In America, the number of children with peanut allergies in 1990 was exceedingly low. Only about four out of a thousand children under the age of eight had a peanut allergy.[132] This meant it was rare for most schools to have more than even one student with a peanut allergy. Despite this, peanuts were banned in schools around the country as they posed an unacceptable risk to these students. The intentions were good – to protect the safety of vulnerable children. Unfortunately, they did the opposite. By 2008, the same survey showed that fourteen out of a thousand children under the age of eight now had a peanut allergy. The rate had more than tripled.

As Haidt points out, the rate increased simply because young children were less exposed to peanuts while growing up. Researchers have definitively proven that deliberately exposing young children to peanuts reduces the likelihood of them developing the allergy later on.[133] The immune system needs to be exposed to potential pathogens in small doses to develop antibodies to fight them. That's how vaccines work. By banning peanuts in schools, more children developed peanut allergies, putting more children at greater risk as they eventually entered the real world. A world where peanuts are not banned because a small proportion of the population is allergic.

That's the beauty of peanuts to Haidt's argument. The parallels are undeniable. Children today are sheltered from any potential risks because parents have their best interests at heart. This culture of safetyism is causing more harm than good for young people. It's important to qualify Haidt's argument as every generation has an old man on a rocking chair making a similar accusation. Specifically, the culture of safetyism he is referring to applies to the generation raised after 1995, the iGen. The arguments apply to this group particularly as the toxic culture now seen on campuses began around 2013, the same time iGen arrived at university.[134]

The majority of iGen who are now on campus have been raised under the parenting style of 'concerted cultivation'. This is the parenting style that most upper to middle-class families used, based on the research of University of Pennsylvania sociologist Annette Lareau.[135] It places emphasis on cultivating a child's talents with a constant focus on cognitive and social development. The child's calendar is constantly scheduled with activities to prepare them for adult life. In contrast, children of working class families usually employ 'natural growth parenting'. This is the style of parenting that assumes children will reach maturity without needing much interference from adults. Children are supervised less and have a lot more unstructured playtime.

The thirty-eight top schools in America, including most Ivy League institutions, had more students from the families in the top 1 percent income bracket than families in the bottom 60 percent.[136] This means that most iGen students on college campuses have been the recipients of a parenting style that makes them the most overparented and overscheduled children of any generation. They grew up where it's too dangerous for a child to walk to school because they might get abducted. It's too dangerous for a child to play with a hammer because they might injure themselves. It's too dangerous for a child to not be invited to a party because their feelings might get hurt. This parenting style evolved because of a genuine concern for the child's physical and emotional safety but it might prove more harmful. It places the children at greater risk as they become adults who are ill-equipped to navigate the stresses of adult life. Like peanuts, young children need to be exposed to small emotional and physical stressors to develop the responses that help protect them against the greater perceived and actual injustices they will invariably experience.

Most middle to upper-class college students are not snowflakes; they have been raised as candles. Fragile beings whose parents have mistakenly attempted to shield them from the winds of adversity.

Instead, "You want to be fire and wish for the wind."

Haidt cites one of my favorite authors, Nassim Nicholas Taleb from his book *Antifragile*.[137] Taleb is not a child psychologist espousing the importance of children not growing up like snowflakes. He is a Lebanese-American scholar of statistical probability as well as a financial trader who predicted the GFC. Taleb probably hates children – he can be like that. His idea of 'antifragile' applies to systems that are the opposite of fragile. They require stressors and challenges to grow otherwise they become weak and inefficient. Like economies, people are antifragile.

This is an indisputable fact as both the human body and mind will atrophy if they are not used. Yet parents, mainly from middle to upper-class families in prosperous countries, treat their children as delicate entities who are easily broken. They need to be emotionally protected at all costs. This has led to students on college campuses lacking the resilience necessary to deal with emotional stress and conflict. It leads to the rise of safe spaces.

Microaggressions are an excellent example of this toxic safetyism culture. A microaggression is a brief verbal or non-verbal exchange that causes intentional or unintentional offense to racial minorities. It's a concept that is widely used on campuses. I googled some examples and found this list from a genuine psychology paper with over 4,000 citations.[138] In the academic world that is like a blue tick on Instagram.

Here is a list of racial microaggressions when said to a person of color:

Where are you from?
You are so articulate.
I believe the most qualified person should get the job.
There is only one race, the human race.

This is a shortlist of the many more microaggressions that you are probably 'guilty of saying'. You can interpret these everyday phrases as offensive and as small acts of aggression – you can interpret them however you like, as Haidt aptly points out. Much of the arts faculty is based on interpreting texts through different lenses. Why as a society would we encourage people to assume the worst possible interpretation of someone's words? There will be cases of people saying things like this from racial prejudice just as there will be cases of people saying it with a genuine desire to connect with people of a different race. Again it's an example of good intentions gone wrong. An attempt to reduce discrimination against racial minorities is a cause that all reasonable people would agree is good thing. But the invention of 'microaggressions' is counterproductive. It creates racial division by making people assume the worst in others. Training students to hear words as aggression and violence is not only disempowering, it's harmful to their mental health.

Some college students now seriously consider words as a form of violence. An article in the *New York Times* in July 2017 was written by a professor of psychology who claimed words were a form of violence.[139] The logic was as follows: words can cause stress; prolonged stress can cause physical harm thus some types of speech are a form of violence. The professor had failed to grasp a basic logical error which Haidt points out.[140] Studying for an exam can cause stress, prolonged stress can cause physical harm thus studying for exams is a form of violence. Everyone knows this is preposterous, but sadly, some higher education facilities teach students to think using this same fallacious argument.

iGen is the most depressed and anxious generation ever.[141] Adolescent depression rates in America have climbed since 2011. By 2016, roughly one out of every five girls reported a major depressive episode the previous year.

Mental health is a serious problem. The attitudes on campus that more safe spaces are needed to combat the mental health epidemic are at odds with the literature on mental health treatment. There is no medical evidence for this view. The idea that people require 'trigger warnings' for sensitive material as they might have had traumatic experiences is the opposite of PTSD treatment. In cognitive behavioral therapy patients are exposed incrementally to the things they find upsetting. The treatment aims to help them become accustomed to the thing they feared so it no longer arouses a fear response. In the words of Haidt, avoiding triggers is a symptom of PTSD not a treatment for it.[142]

The culture of safetyism is harmful. If young people are taught that words are violence, then they will feel threatened whenever they disagree with someone. They will be vulnerable to the words of any stranger who could make them feel harmed by so much as opening their mouth. It is an empowering mindset to realize that we can control our thoughts and emotions. We can choose how we respond to words. Either we choose to be offended or not, this is stoic philosophy.

The world is a dangerous place, filled with people and countries that wish physical violence upon us. There are people who want to control how we think so they can manipulate us for their personal gain. This is happening to us right now. Unless the next generation of young people are armed with the tools to be resilient, able to argue and engage with ideas, then there are grave dangers for our society. Truth is the only lantern we have to illuminate the darkness that power, suffering and deceit all occupy.

The truth can never hurt.

DR CORNEL WEST

16. RACE AND LOVE MATTER

TOPIC: AMERICA
GUEST: PHILOSOPHER
PODCAST: #1325
WHERE TO FIND MORE: RACE MATTERS (BOOK)

The ancient city of Athens. Home of democracy, white tunics, orgies, wine, deceit and politics. Words held great power here as students studied the art of rhetoric; how to speak persuasively. Many powerful men were made from standing in an amphitheater and convincing their fellow citizens of their agenda. It was a city of words and if they didn't work, it was a city of blood.

In 430 B.C., Athens was at the peak of its power. It had a military hegemony over neighboring states which formed the Athenian empire and there was also great emphasis placed on the arts as literature, sculpture, philosophy and architecture prospered. It was a golden age by all accounts.

No doubt its citizens were full of pride as their social experiment of democracy and empire flourished. Men in white tunics would meet in public places such as the famous Agora to discuss politics and trade – but it was not an egalitarian society where everyone was of equal status. Far from it. There were well to do aristocrats who looked down on the common man: the baker, the farmer or the fisherman. It was a city of fierce ambition as people sought to climb the social ladder, drink at important parties and eat with important men.

Then there was a man called Socrates. A philosopher who lived in the city of Athens at this time and one who would leave an indelible mark on the rest of history. Why has everyone heard of this ancient Athenian?

Socrates would walk around the city barefoot, unwashed and unruly. He would go up to any man in the city regardless of their status or wealth and ask them questions. Nothing was off- limits as he challenged every treasured belief people held. How do you know this? Can you give me an example of that? Are these reasons good enough?

It made Socrates a despised yet famous man. Self-important elites were outraged that they had to justify their often unjustifiable beliefs. They viewed him as a threat, a man who would corrupt Athenian youth, teaching them immoral values. His questions were dangerous.

In 399 B.C., the questioning became too much, Socrates was charged and faced trial. This became the most famous court hearing in the history of Western civilization.

In front of a jury of five hundred of his fellow citizens, Socrates would have to defend himself against the charges of corrupting the youth and not believing in the Greek Gods. Once again this was a battle of words. In his monologue he delivered the now famous line:

"The unexamined life is not worth living."[143]

Socrates was found guilty and sentenced to death. His loyal followers had devised numerous escape routes for the old philosopher but he was content to accept the punishment given to him by his people. He drank his hemlock and died.

Fast forward a few thousand years and instead of white tunics and ancient Athenians, there is another great democracy with a vast empire, the American Empire. Instead of Socrates, another great philosopher is questioning the entire system itself.

Joe Rogan's next guest is none other than Dr Cornel West, arguably the most famous African American philosopher and public intellectual of the 21st century. An activist and fierce defender of the rights of the downtrodden, his own stated goal is to:

"question the soul of America."

It's really unsurprising that for his appearance on the podcast he quotes Socrates, "the unexamined life is not worth living." Just like Socrates, Dr West is willing to question powerful structures that would prefer blind obedience, denouncing greed and materialism and questioning everything. Every empire has a dark history that its citizens prefer to overlook. America's dark history is black history, the history of African Americans and the American Empire. Dr Cornel West refuses to be silent.

A master orator himself, West's voice is rich with the rhythm of a jazz musician, the passion of a preacher, and the vocabulary of a Harvard professor (which he is). His ideas are powerful and his 2019 appearance on the podcast is more relevant than ever in 2020.

For eight minutes and forty-six seconds, a police officer pressed his foot on the neck of George Floyd resulting in his death in Minneapolis. "I can't breathe," Floyd muttered as he gasped for air. A video of Floyd's death ignited the country as protests occurred in every major city in America. The Black Lives Matter movement had a resurgence in the public eye. Social media influencers were quick to show their support for the movement with carefully curated posts on how to be 'anti-racist' calling out others not as woke as them. Old TV shows with performers in blackface were removed from streaming sites and corporations posted #BlackLivesMatter.

But does any of this address the problem of systemic racism? What does systemic racism actually mean? Unlike corporations and influencers, Dr West has been involved in the civil rights movement before there was a hashtag. His book *Race Matters* is an authoritative work on the racial struggles of black Americans. Dr West's perspective on race is one which everyone needs to hear, especially now.

So how did we get to this point?

Before Dr West answers this, he always starts from a place of love. Something missing from many of the heated discussions at the moment. It is a deep-rooted love of humanity where he addresses everyone as brother or sister – including brother Trump. Dr Cornel West does not seek to divide people over their differences or condemn individuals for their past but instead he seeks to bring people together. He does not hate people because they disagree with him, or try to get their shows canceled, or take the moral high ground. In his own words,

> "Brother Trump is a gangster. I was a gangster before I met Jesus and now I am a redeemed sinner with gangster proclivities. So I know what I'm talking about."

Anyone who publicly owns their flaws before addressing the flaws of others is usually someone you can trust. This message of bringing people together through our humanity does not just extend to our flaws but also to our greatest triumphs as a species. Music, comedy and literature. Dr West's philosophy is inseparable from culture as he brings people in through a collective love of the arts.

Whether it be Richard Pryor, the father of stand-up comedy who taught America how to laugh at itself, or Aretha Franklin whose voice could bring tears to even the sternest of faces. America's rich soul can be found on stages and bars, in libraries and cinemas, and even on street corners. That soul is indistinguishable from the African American community who have been at the center of culture for much of America's history.

Yet this soul of America is tainted. The nation was built on the backs of slaves as the Atlantic slave trade saw more than 12 million Africans shipped across the ocean over 400 years. Slavery was the economic engine for most of the Southern States. Southern slave owners had tobacco, cotton and sugar cane plantations that profited directly from slave labor. The slave trade created more millionaires per capita in the Mississippi River valley than anywhere else in the nation.[144] The Southern States relied on slavery for economic growth. It became so embedded into their way of life that the South was willing to leave the United States for their 'right' to own and trade slaves. This led to the Civil War in 1861.

The Northern States defeated the South and in 1863 Abraham Lincoln enacted the great emancipation of all slaves in America.

> "that all persons held as slaves" within the rebellious states "are, and henceforward shall be free."[145]

The struggle for black freedom did not end here. A century of marginalization followed as the South enacted Jim Crow laws that saw the segregation of white and black Americans. These cunningly designed laws used literacy tests, taxes and grandfather clauses to take away the voting rights of black citizens. They worked. In 1900, there were zero African Americans registered to vote in North Carolina and this trend was seen all over the South. These laws extended into every facet of life and made obtaining a good education, getting a good job and accumulating wealth almost impossible. By alienating African Americans from the economic system, communities were left in poverty. The shackles of slavery had been removed only to be replaced by a less visible form of bondage.

In 1964, over a hundred years after emancipation, the Civil Rights Act was passed. It was the result of one of the greatest marches on Washington in American history where remarkable leaders such as Martin Luther King Jr, Rosa Parks and Bayard Rustin led a peaceful protest to gain equal rights for the black community. It was a monumental achievement that made discrimination based on race unlawful.

So how, more than fifty years later, did we get to this point where there is more civil unrest than ever? How did George Floyd's death ignite a racial fire that had been waiting to explode?

Why is there a racial crisis in America?

According to Dr West, the fundamental crisis is that there is too much poverty in the black community.[146] West details the changing employment landscape for African Americans. The structural shift in the economy away from the manufacturing sector to the service sector has benefited the highly educated middle and upper classes. This shift has been disastrous for African Americans who have been priced out of good high schools and expensive colleges. Unskilled workers have had their wages driven below what is needed to live a life of decency. This has been compounded by the increasing mechanization of Southern agriculture, with less human labor now required to do the same job. Sixty years ago, 50 percent of all black teenagers had agricultural jobs and more than 90 percent of those workers lived in the South.[147] These jobs have long since been in decline and that has led to a mass exodus from the farms to the cities. With few employment prospects, there are now significant numbers of people excluded from the economy who reside in urban dwellings, with no chance of gaining the skills needed for employment. In 1980, 15 percent of black men between the ages of twenty-five and forty-six reported earning not one cent the previous year. These statistics remain similar even today. The sheer lack of hope and opportunity is the essential ingredient for crime as drugs provide a source of income that doesn't require a degree. Herein lies the tragic cycle of poverty. Police target those living in impoverished urban areas with a higher crime rate; the more police, the more incarceration. Even though black people consume 12 percent of the drugs they account for 70 percent of drug convictions.[148] This is a natural product of putting more police in predominately black neighborhoods. If you put more police in fraternities, you would expect more frat boys to be arrested. As more young black men are placed in jail, more children are left without fathers to raise them and provide income to the family. Single motherhood is the biggest predictor of child poverty.[149] And when there is a 1 in 4 chance that a black man born today will spend time in prison[150], it should be of little surprise that the poverty cycle continues. The overt forms of racism in the past have been replaced with less obvious forms of institutional racism. Sometimes what it takes is a video to expose to the world just how real and overt this discrimination actually is.

Hashtags and cancellation culture will not solve this problem. The best quote that Dr West makes is the following:

> "To engage in serious discussions about race we must not begin with the problems of black people but the flaws of American society."[151]

The flaws are a free market economy that emphasizes profit and not people. Corporations can post #BlackLivesMatter despite their reliance on cheap labor from poorer countries that devalue working-class wages domestically. This disproportionately affects African Americans who have the highest rate of poverty in America at 27.4 percent. Civil unrest is a product of having one part of the community deliberately excluded by the economic system and punished by the judicial system. These two forces accelerate a poverty cycle that has catastrophic impacts for the people within it. Comedians, artists and singers are forces against the soulless engine of capitalism. Whether through laughter or pain, they send the message that the crisis of black America needs to be addressed. Not through hashtags and woke posts but changes to the engine itself. Dave Chappelle is one of these voices.

If the unexamined life is not worth living, then the unexamined society is not worth living in. Dr West provides an analysis of the racial crisis in America which is a product of poverty and all the despair that goes with it. Symbols will not change America, only structural change which reduces the gross income inequality and poverty within the black community. Race matters. But messages on race that do not start with love are destined to end in hate.

If only people would take heed of the words of the great Martin Luther King Jr.

DARKNESS CANNOT DRIVE OUT DARKNESS; ONLY LIGHT CAN DO THAT. HATE CANNOT DRIVE OUT HATE; ONLY LOVE CAN DO THAT.

SAM HARRIS

17. THE SELF IS AN ILLUSION

TOPIC: MINDFULNESS
GUEST: NEUROSCIENTIST
PODCAST: #192, #410, #543, #641, #804 +
WHERE TO FIND MORE: WAKING UP (BOOK)

A middle-aged man is locked in a closet. He sits with his legs crossed and his eyes closed. The man has been in the closet for three months. There are no books, movies or other people to talk to. Food will occasionally be placed outside the closet and the man will be allowed to eat before he returns to what he was doing, which was nothing. Absolutely nothing. To most human beings this solitary confinement would be considered a form of torture. The prospect of being left alone in an elevator with one's own mind for just a minute is scary enough. The thought of three months with only ourselves as company is terrifying. The person inside our head would drive us literally insane.

This man chose to be in this closet. He was searching for something although there was quite literally nothing there. What was there to find in an empty damp room? What could be worth leaving your family and friends behind for months of nothingness? It seems almost self-destructive. How could one possibly explain to someone at a party that they intended to do this? It would be easier to say to someone that you intended to do a lot of acid and stay in your room for an indefinite amount of time. The man in the closet was not using any drugs. The man was none other than the famous neuroscientist, philosopher and skeptic, Sam Harris. He had embarked on a three-month meditation retreat.

Why did one of the world's leading skeptics and critics of religion embark on this three-month closet expedition? And more importantly, how was he capable of this incredible level of mental fortitude? I had seen a few other people display a similar level of mental resilience before. There were monks capable of walking over hot coals, runners who could run further in one go than most people could drive and people who could withstand arctic sea-water in their underpants. There seemed to be this mysterious level of consciousness that people were tapping into to accomplish impossible feats. How were these people reaching into the depths of their minds?

To find the answer to this question, I went on my own virtual pilgrimage through e-books, podcasts and my neuroscience textbook. I stumbled upon Sam's book called *Waking Up*. A rather controversial title implying that most of us were 'asleep' in our day to day lives. If there was a product I could buy to become 'woke' I would almost certainly purchase it. It seemed Sam was saying he was Morpheus and everyone else was Neo. Take the red pill and your conscious experience will be liberated. Sadly, there was no pill or product to achieve this state for longer than a few hours. There was only an idea which could offer a heightened state of consciousness forever.

To liberate your consciousness, you have to realize you don't exist. The self is an illusion, Harris said on the podcast. Rogan looked stumped. It seemed absurd – how could thinking I don't exist, help me walk across hot coals? In a world of uncertainty, the only certainty seems to be that we exist. It's the only conclusion every human independently arrives at. We all exist in our heads. "I think, therefore I am," Descartes famously said. The 17th century philosopher was certain of nothing other than his own existence after questioning every fundamental piece of knowledge he held. So when I first heard Sam Harris say this on the podcast,[152] I wanted to cite the whole of human experience as a rebuttal. But as you will soon find out, my arguments did not hold up. We don't exist. At least not in the way that most of us think we do.

To appreciate the argument, it helps to first consider what consciousness is – it's a question that philosophers, scientists and stoners have grappled with for centuries. Consciousness seems to be the control seat of our existence. The person living inside our head. Sam goes into great depth in his book about the intellectual landscape of consciousness but this can often leave one more confused than when they started. The best representation of consciousness that I have read comes from the famous psychologist, Jonathan Haidt in his book, *The Happiness Hypothesis.* He uses the metaphor of a tiny rider sitting on top of a large elephant to explain how the mind works.[153] The rider represents the conscious part of our brain. This includes the processes over which we have a degree of control such as language-based thinking. The elephant is everything else that goes on in the brain. These are the automatic processes that we are not consciously aware of – which are most things. Right now you are not aware of the hormones your mind is ordering your body to secrete or the messages your brain is sending to maintain your homeostatic function or a thousand other complex chemical processes. We simply aren't aware of most things that are going on in our subconscious minds. We are the small riders on top of enormous elephants who think we are in control. We think we choose the path the elephant takes when the elephant is immeasurably stronger than the rider. If there is disagreement between the rider and elephant, the elephant will choose where the rider goes. If the elephant decides to go left, the rider will have a million reasons for why left was the best choice when in reality, he didn't even get to choose. Psychological research shows that the 'rider' is extremely skilled at producing post-hoc justifications for what the 'elephant' chooses to do.[154] The conscious brain seems to be playing catch up for what the unconscious brain has already done.

But if we look closer, the rider doesn't even exist according to Harris. The subjective experience of consciousness is nothing more than an illusion. There is no place in your brain where 'you' exist. Many people assume there is a specific part of the brain where the rider lives, the person who is in control of the mind. There might just be no evidence to support this commonly held view. If you look closely enough at the elephant and the rider, you will start to see the rider disappear like a mirage in the desert. The elephant is all there is. The sense of being a self, an ego, is an illusion.

This idea that the self is an illusion is the type of idea you hear late at night from someone who is usually incredibly high and incredibly uninformed. Sam Harris is a neuroscientist who has been fixated on the nature of consciousness for a long time. His argument that the self does not exist is grounded in the lack of neuro-anatomical evidence for the self-existing. If we are to believe Harris, it is useful to think about what evidence would prove his claim wrong. If neuroscience could prove the 'rider' exists by having an image of the brain showing a single part is activated during conscious processes, then Harris would be discredited. In simple words, if there is a rider, he must have a bedroom in the brain. This is why his most damning evidence, in my view, comes from the famous split-brain experiments. These show that there is not a single point in the brain where consciousness can exist. He provides very little detail of the experiment but luckily I have a big fat neuroscience textbook to help explain.

Our brains can be split into two halves. The left and right hemispheres. Connecting these two hemispheres is a bundle of nerve fibers called the corpus callosum. The corpus callosum allows for communication between both sides of the brain. In the 1960s, Roger Sperry studied humans with such extreme epilepsy that their corpus callosum was severed as a last-resort treatment.[155] This stopped the patient's seizures but had some other consequences. The separation meant these people effectively had two brains as the wires connecting both hemispheres had been cut: a left brain and a right brain. Roger Sperry discovered you could show these patients an image and while they wouldn't be able to articulate what it was, they could still recognize it. The two brains couldn't communicate but were still aware in different ways of what the image was. For example, you could show the patient an image of a pen in their left visual field. The right hemisphere processes the left visual field. The right brain. When these patients were asked what they saw, they could not say the words yet they could reach for a pen in their pocket and tell you it was the same thing as the image they saw. They were consciously aware of the pen, but they couldn't articulate what it was.

As Harris explores, the split-brain experiments pose a big problem for those who believe that consciousness can be located in the brain. This is because when the brain is divided into two, both halves operate as if the other half doesn't exist. Each half is technically conscious. So there could be two separate places of consciousness. Our left brain, which is largely responsible for language, simply might not be able to articulate the right brain's conscious experience. Harris points out we could all be like Roger Sperry's patients who are simply unable to verbalize things they are undoubtedly aware of.[156] Think of all the thoughts you might be having without 'you' even realizing.

The feeling that consciousness is one unified experience is challenged when consciousness can be divided into physical points.[157] This is scientific evidence that the sense of being one static entity is no more than an illusion.

The idea that consciousness is anything other than a subjective illusion is challenged by science and basic thought experiments. Are you the same person you were ten years ago? The cells in our bodies are constantly replicating with every cell replaced about every ten years. This means you are made up of a set of entirely new cells from the old version of yourself. So how much of you is the same? It seems like the passenger in our mind is the only thing which has not changed.

Unfortunately, Harris shows how this too can be shown to be false. He poses the following thought experiment which was originally devised by Derek Parfit.[158] Imagine there is a teleportation device that could take you to Mars. As soon as a green button is pressed you appear on the surface of Mars. But there is a catch. The teleportation device must terminate the copy of you on Earth for you to exist on Mars. You will be the exact same person with every single memory right up until the green button was pressed. Are you still the same person on the surface of Mars? Most people say no. Even if someone is given the exact same memories, thoughts, genes and double chin as us, they are not us. What if you take away someone's memories? Are they still the same conscious person? People with relatives who have Alzheimer's disease would hope so. This means there is no fixed concept of self carried along from one moment to the next. The only thing that makes you, you is the feeling of being you. In the words of Harris, "Duplicate your brain and you will duplicate the contents of your brain in another field of consciousness."[159] The rider is nothing more than the subjective experience of riding the elephant. But you are the elephant.

If you are still not convinced that the self is an illusion, read the book, and you will be. But now it's time to answer our initial question. What do those who can walk on hot coals, run ultramarathons and endure arctic cold waters have in common? While I cannot claim to have achieved any of these feats, many guests on the podcast have. They all talk about a level of focus so intense that everything else other than the present moment disappears. The internal monologue goes away; the sense of being a self is gone. Interestingly this is the same state of consciousness that many spiritual leaders have talked about for thousands of years. The skeptics among us will be keen to dismiss this mystic talk as nothing more than fiction. But this state of heightened consciousness can be achieved by anyone through the secular practice of meditation and mindfulness. A state of mind so powerful that regular practice can alter the grey matter in our brain.[160] It seems only now the Western world of psychology is listening to the eastern world of spirituality.

Yongey Mingyur Rinpoche, is a Tibetan teacher who provides a useful analogy for how we can practice mindfulness to pierce the illusion of self. It is all about awareness. Our awareness exists even if we are not aware of it. Awareness is like space. It is just there. Our thoughts and emotions are like clouds that pass through the space. Most people exist constantly floating in the clouds of emotion being tugged whichever way the clouds wish to go. Alex Jones is a great example. If Alex Jones feels angry, he becomes angry. If Alex Jones feels worried, he becomes worried. Mindfulness or meditation is the practice of being aware of these clouds as they pass through your consciousness. The process of being aware that you are not your emotions. If Sam feels angry, he is aware that the emotion has arisen in his consciousness but he does not then become angry. He is not continually hijacked by thoughts and emotions. This is the goal of meditation. To escape the illusion of the self which is persistently deluded by its thoughts and emotions. The rider of the elephant can get distressed because the elephant is not going the way he wants. Or he can simply realize that the elephant will choose where he goes and he only has control over his response to where he is going. Mindfulness is the power of not being at the mercy of external things that we can't control.

Some people might interpret this as wacky philosophy with little practical benefit. At least it's how I felt when I initially engaged with it. But after actually trying the practice it became clear how little control I had over my mind. One Facebook comment could hijack my thoughts for hours. Clearly I had a lot to learn. The science is also clear. Meditation has a multitude of positive effects. It has been shown to reduce depression, stress, and anxiety – and increase our capacity to withstand physical pain.[161] But embarking on meditation for health benefits is like having sex to get a cardiovascular workout. It's not the point. The point is to explore the uncharted territories of consciousness and liberate yourself from the emotions and thoughts which imprison you.

The self is an illusion that causes unnecessary suffering.

CAMERON HANES

18. HUNTING IS ETHICAL

TOPIC: HUNTING
GUEST: ATHLETE
PODCAST: #450, #567, #759, #815, #944 +
WHERE TO FIND MORE:
BACKCOUNTRY BOWHUNTING (BOOK)

A baby antelope grazes on some shrubs on the African savannah. Its legs are thin – like miniature stilts. Its small but wide eyes are cute like Bambi's. The antelope sees a blade of grass that looks especially nice to eat.

The animal wanders away from its mum and dad for a brief second, making its way to the outskirts of the herd. Never before has the antelope tasted grass so delicious. It takes another step away.

The antelope's mother scans the horizon. She can sense her offspring is not by her side. Frantically she looks to see where the baby antelope has ventured to. She sees it. Her baby is happily eating some grass on the periphery of the herd.

Something else is watching the baby antelope. A lioness. The female lion is lying down in a thicket of grass, hidden from sight. Like an athlete on the starting blocks, she's waiting for the signal. As soon as the baby antelope takes one step further, it will be time.

The baby antelope takes another step.

The lioness propels her body from the thicket of grass onto the open plain. Instantly, the herd begins to run as they sense the predator. The larger antelope elegantly bound off into the distance. But the lioness is fast.

The baby antelope is trying to run as fast it can, its skinny legs gallop awkwardly. Its mum and dad turn around to see it being chased by the lioness. Within seconds, the lioness is a breath away. She pounces, burying her teeth into the jugular of the baby antelope. There is a moment of resistance before the creature takes its last breath and says goodbye to the world.

The parents take one last look before they bound off into the distance, never to see their calf again.

The lioness takes the antelope back to its pride. The adult lions take their share. Then the young cubs tear into the remains, savoring every piece of meat in their mouths. After an hour of feasting, the sun begins to set. And the hyenas have grown impatient.

The pack of hyenas encircle the lions, snarling like dogs. They have waited for too long. There are too many hyenas for the lions to put up a fight. They give up the kill reluctantly and, as they walk away, they roar to make sure their dominance is not forgotten. The lion is the king of the savannah but it knows when to walk away.

The hyenas feast on the remains. A dozen muzzles competing for even a mouthful of meat. Within minutes, there is almost nothing left. The scavengers hurry away in pursuit of the next carcass they can strip bare.

All alone, the baby antelope's mutilated corpse remains. Above it, the vultures are circling high in the sky – they too have been waiting their turn. Now the hyenas are gone, they descend. First they take the eyes. Then they diligently pick at every last bit of flesh until bones are all that's left.

The next idea is that hunting is ethical. This controversial idea can change the way you live your life. It changed Joe Rogan's life and the lives of many fans of the podcast. Before we unpack this idea, why did I tell a story of a baby animal being viciously killed and eaten?

In the modern world, people buy their food from supermarkets. One magical location that houses every type of meat, vegetable and fruit you could possibly want. Everything is prepared and ready for you, with the only challenge being opening your wallet and tapping your credit card. Not many people give much thought to how the sausages, bacon, steaks and ribs in their basket actually got there. It's not something we want to think about. Most people walking through the aisles of the supermarket have never killed an animal in their life. But they have almost certainly eaten one. In North America around 13 percent of people think it is unacceptable to hunt for your own meat.[162] Yet only 5 percent of the population is vegan or vegetarian. This leaves a subset of the population who eat meat yet, strangely, are critical of people who hunt to get meat for themselves. A further 28 percent of people surveyed think it is unacceptable to hunt to control animal population. Hunting was also viewed especially poorly among young people. This suggests the next generation of Americans will not be huge fans of hunting.

Humans have become so removed from the process of food production that people in the 21st century are willing to criticize people who kill for their own meat to eat, while they implicitly condone industrialized slaughterhouses which kill to provide meat for them. Pictures of a hunter with a slain baby antelope evoke outrage, but pictures of veal on a supermarket shelf evoke relief as a meal the whole family can eat. Stories of animal suffering move us; most people don't like seeing animals suffer. But sadly, people's ignorance about where their food comes from and the selective compassion that entails, causes more harm than good. Many can be guilty of this ignorance in a world where most people live in urban populations - hopelessly separated from wild, natural landscapes like the savannahs of Africa or backcountry Alaska. It's easy to forget the animal kingdom is brutal, babies get torn away from their parents and eaten. The weak of the herd are left to die. But death is essential to survival; the carcass of an animal is recycled by all the other animals in that ecosystem. The meat of a baby antelope feeds a baby lion. This is the harshness of the circle of life. Death gives way to life.

A man who understands the circle of life better than most humans alive is Cameron Hanes. He exists in it. Hanes will navigate some of the most treacherous terrains in pursuit of big game to hunt. Deep in the wilderness, where cries for help cannot be heard, Hanes will track game up mountains in winter snow or summer heat. Often, he will do this by himself. He is not armed with a rifle or shotgun but, instead, a bow and arrow. This requires an exceptional degree of stealth to get within range of an animal – animals that have fled from predators for as long as their species have existed. But Cameron Hanes is the ultimate predator. The world's best bow hunter did not obtain this title by chance or skill alone. Hanes trains harder than most mainstream athletes, running a marathon a day as well as an intensive weights program. He does this so that when he is within range he can kill the animal cleanly, and with precision. Whether it be elk from Oregon or caribou from Canada, with Hanes aiming the bow, it usually is just a second of suffering before death arrives.

When he talks to Rogan, it becomes abundantly clear, hunting is not just a thrill; it's something with a spiritual level of importance. I have never heard someone at Walmart say the same thing about buying their steak so, naturally, I was interested. Why do hunters hunt? And how can hunting be ethical?

The reason that most hunters hunt is for the meat.[163] Behind each set of deer antlers mounted on a wall was a meat supply that could have lasted for almost a year. This is wild game meat devoid of processing, additives and preservatives. It's 100 percent natural. Hanes and Rogan both talk about the immense satisfaction of providing your family with food from an animal you have chased up a mountain, looked in the eye and shot with an arrow. To some this might seem cruel, but one only needs to take a visit to a slaughterhouse to see how most animals are killed to provide the meat that arrives on your plate.

Cattle are marched into the slaughterhouse. One by one they come down a walkway and into a squeezing chute, the metal cage presses against their sides, allowing no wriggle room.

An employee on an elevated platform will take aim with a metal apparatus called a CASH knocker. The device shoots a blank shell against the animal's head that is supposed to render it unconscious. Then it will be suspended by a chain that goes around its hind leg and the large blood vessels in the neck are cut so it bleeds out over a drain. Not all animals will be knocked out by the CASH knocker and about one in a hundred cows will moan in agony as they are still aware of what is happening to them.[164] Everyone would prefer to not know how their meat gets to them but unless the truth is confronted, the ethics of hunting are not fully appreciated.

Hunting gives the animal a chance to evade death. An unskilled hunter will not be able to track and kill an animal. In this sense it restores balance to the circle of life and death that is hopelessly absent from animals bred to make the walk into the squeezing chute. Meat is an important part of the human diet and hunting services this need while also keeping animals in their natural habitat instead of the artificial environments we construct for them.

Hunters are also important conservationists. This might seem like a paradox but hunters across the world play an important role in conserving natural habitats. They are one of the few groups who routinely go into the great outdoors and lobby to keep it pristine. In fact, *National Geographic* ran an article that showed hunting lobbies played a vital role in preserving outdoor landscapes in Washington State, North Dakota, South Carolina and the Western States.[165] One example is Ducks Unlimited, a non-profit organization of hunters, who have saved 13 million acres of waterfowl habitat throughout North America. The group is arguably more effective than most other environmental lobby groups in America. Not surprisingly, as people spending a lot of time in the outdoors, they want to preserve it as opposed to allowing commercial interests to exploit public land. Ironically, the most vocal groups against the cruelty of hunters usually share a similar stance with them on the environment. It could be a point of unity not division.

Cameron Hanes often uploads pictures of dead animals to his Instagram which causes the occasional outcry and online backlash. This speaks to the dark side of hunting, trophy hunting.

In 2015, Cecil the lion was killed by the American dentist, Walter Palmer. Photos of the dead lion garnered international attention. People were outraged and rightfully so. Lions are an endangered species and they are rarely used for meat. Instead, international hunters pay thousands of dollars to come to Africa and kill these majestic cats only to showcase the head as a trophy. Carol Baskin and Doc Antle are the kind of people we are talking about. My grandfather was a game ranger in Kruger National Park, South Africa and nothing would have upset him more than a fat guy who shot a lion and then paraded around with its skin. It's disgusting. But as with everything in Africa, the industry of trophy hunting is more complex than the media usually cares to show, and, ethically, it is a murky swamp to enter.

Cameron Hanes is not a trophy hunter; he eats the animals he kills or hunts animals with unsafe population growth such as bears in North America. But as the face of the hunting game, he is willing to discuss the ethics of the darker sides of the community he loves. Trophy hunting in Africa involves people from around the world coming to the continent in pursuit of big game to kill. It's very expensive. The cost to kill a lion ranges from US$50,000 to US$75,000. To kill an elephant costs between

US$40,000 to US$73,000.[166] Hunters will often use tracking dogs and state of the art equipment including laser scopes and high powered rifles. In South Africa alone it is a US$100 million industry. No arguments can be made about how these hunters are a part of the circle of life. They stay at hunting farms where the animals have been bred to be killed, not much better than animals bred to be eaten. Western backlash has sought to stop this indulgent and often narcissistic form of trophy hunting. But this is having an unexpected cost. In impoverished African countries, it's easy to impose Western morals from afar. The simple fact is these industries provide the only source of employment for the many locals involved. In addition, trophy hunters are forced by law to spend huge money on building up local communities. The big game animals have become an economic asset, so it is in the communities' interest to protect them. In fact, each elephant shot by a trophy hunter pays for the conservation of 2,500 other elephants.[167]

It's a twisted economic argument that speaks to how perverted the world can be sometimes. The only way to save an elephant is to assign it an economic value and let the free market do the rest. The pros and cons of trophy hunting are very complicated and somewhat disheartening.

But the murky waters of trophy hunting should not obscure the ethics of people hunting non-endangered species for their own meat or for population control. Cameron Hanes is not only an advocate for hunting, he is an advocate for reconnecting with our humanity.

By placing ourselves at the whim of nature, we are in the same circle of life and death that all other animals live in. Hunting for your own meat gives a purpose to life that you will not find aimlessly wandering through supermarket aisles.

It might seem dangerous but it is a world we all long to rejoin. In the words of Cameron Hanes:

"Keep hammering."

ROBERT SAPOLSKY

19. HUMANS DON'T HAVE FREE WILL

TOPIC: BEHAVIOR
GUEST: NEUROENDOCRINOLOGIST
PODCAST: #965
WHERE TO FIND MORE: BEHAVE (BOOK)

On a warm summer's day in August, 1966, Charles Whitman looked out from the main tower's observation deck at the University of Texas. It is a campus I have been lucky enough to walk around. The view would have been beautiful as the Texas sun shone over the students moving around campus. Whitman would have had panoramic views of students walking to classes for philosophy, engineering and medicine. Then he aimed his rifle. In the following ninety minutes he killed fourteen people and injured thirty-one others. At that time, it was the largest mass shooting by a lone gunman in U.S. history.

Charles Whitman was a former marine with an IQ of 140 who had been on a scholarship to study mechanical engineering at the university. In his suicide note Whitman requested that the authorities complete an autopsy on his body to see if they could discern the cause of his increasing headaches and violent urges. The autopsy was completed and revealed a brain tumor the size of a pecan pressing against Whitman's amygdala.[168] This is the region of the brain most linked to aggression and fear responses. Was Charles Whitman in control of his actions? Or was there a greater biological force operating? In other words, do humans have free will or is everything we do pre-determined?

Robert Sapolsky's answer to this question may destabilize not only your view of right and wrong but also the very foundations of the criminal justice system. Sapolsky is a neuroendocrinologist at Stanford University and considered a leading authority on neuroscience and the behavior of primates. He believes the concept of free will does not exist. Free will is the ability to make a voluntary decision that is not determined by prior causes or divine intervention. Free will is what enables man to choose between actions that are right and wrong. Free will is the very essence of the American dream. And it doesn't exist according to Sapolsky.

Many Western readers will want to stop reading at this point. Such a statement must be bullshit. You intuitively know that free will exists. After all, how can humans possibly not have control over their choices? What would be the point of doing anything? Everything would be pointless and we'd just sit back and watch as fate slowly takes us to our graves.

There is an array of internal biological forces that influence our decision-making process without us consciously realizing. For example, if you place a cold cup in someone's hand and then ask them to judge someone's character for the first time, they are more likely to view the person as cold and unfriendly.[169] And if you ask them about their ability to judge character they are likely to tell you they are fairly accurate yet they just formed an opinion dictated by a cup of ice water.

A useful metaphor for how the brain works is provided by Sapolsky. There are three layers. The first layer is our automatic, regulatory system. This layer controls our breathing, blood glucose levels and many other things we do not need to think about. The second layer is the limbic system. This is a complex set of structures largely responsible for human emotion. The final layer, the neocortex, is our most recently evolved and is responsible for cognition and memory. It is in the neocortex, where most of the processes we associate with being 'conscious' occur. This is where our beloved free will can be exercised. All we need to do is use our powerful neocortex to override our ancient monkey brains.

Wrong. The neocortex is not the divine ruler of our minds. Instead there is a bidirectional relationship whereby the limbic system can influence the neocortex and vice versa. Your emotions can influence your cognition before you have time to think. This is because information is processed by the limbic system two hundred times faster than our cognitive brain. Our ancestors didn't have time to philosophize about the intentions of a lion; they had to run away instantly. Their instinctual emotion of fear caused them to run away before they could think about why they should be fearful. Our 'free will' is beholden to these often uncontrollable emotional states. Indeed, much of rationality seems to explain the moral conclusions we had already arrived at. Reason is just playing catch up to our emotions. Have you ever made a decision based on a gut feeling instead of the facts? Neuroscience can explain this.

In the prefrontal cortex where cognition occurs, there are two key functional structures. These are the dorsolateral prefrontal cortex (DLPFC) and the ventromedial prefrontal cortex (VMPFC). Sapolsky goes into tremendous detail about the neuroscience in his book and very little in the podcast. A middle ground is needed to understand these parts of the brain and how they relate to free will. The DLPFC is the rational, unsentimental, utilitarian part of decision making. It's like a politician who is willing to kill one to save five. Its decision making is based on cold reason with no emotions. The VMPFC is the emotional part of decision making and is an honorary member of the limbic system. It works by thinking about how an outcome would make us feel and then comes to a conclusion. When asked a moral question such as, "Would you intentionally kill someone to save five others?" Most people say no. Amazingly these moral questions all activate our limbic system and the VMPFC first. The VMPFC makes us consider how we would feel about intentionally killing someone – we don't feel too good about it so we would prefer to let five people die from our inaction. It is this emotion that we feel in our gut that informs many of our decisions. The DLPFC activates after a delay and is used to rationalize the conclusion which has already been made. If someone has damage to their VMPFC, their moral decision making becomes almost psychopathically detached and hyper-rational. They are willing to kill a close family member to save five strangers for example.[170]

How can we as humans claim to have free will when our emotions can make decisions for us? The most damning study showed that knowing a judge's opinion on Kant, Nietzsche and utilitarianism philosophy does not predict how long a sentence would be more accurately than knowing how hungry they were. Judges would hand out their longest sentences just before lunch.[171] It's easy to imagine a judge giving an elaborate speech on the need for the rule of law while they sentenced someone to life imprisonment when in reality, their thinking was influenced by the need to eat a jelly bean.

The most famous experiment which challenged the idea of free will is the Libet experiment. Here people were asked to lift up their right or left finger. It was their choice. The only parameter was that they must note the time they consciously decided to pick left or right. During the experiment they were connected to an EEG machine that recorded the electrical activity in their brain. It specifically monitored the activation of neurons in the secondary motor cortex – the part of the brain involved in lifting a finger. Incredibly the signal to lift a finger up was sent before people noted their conscious decision. Their brain knew the left finger was going to be lifted before they did.

Before we proceed, it should be noted that Robert Sapolsky is one of the few guests that Rogan actually left his studio to interview. This should say something about the quality of this man and his ideas. Many of his lectures at Stanford are free online and cover a breadth of topics in a devilishly articulate way. Humans not having free will is a minor focus of his recent book *Behave* but one in which he goes into great detail in the podcast.[172] The following evidence for humans not having free will comes directly from some of his own research. It is terrifying. It involves cat piss, motorbikes and parasites.

There is a parasite called toxoplasmosis (toxo) which can only reproduce in a cat's stomach. The cat excretes the toxo in its feces. Rodents then eat the feces. Remarkably, the toxo in these feces now hijacks the rodent's behavior for its own benefit. The toxo is on a mission for the rodent to be eaten by a cat so it can reproduce and prosper in the cat's stomach. As a result, it rewires the rodent's brain to make it attracted to the smell of cat urine. This increases the likelihood of the rat being eaten by a cat and the toxo parasite finding its way to the stomach where it can reproduce.

What makes this so remarkable is that rodents are innately afraid of cat urine. You can take a rat that has been bred in a laboratory for five thousand generations and it still displays this innate fear response. Somehow, toxo can locate the precise neural pathway in the rat's amygdala and rewire it to do the exact opposite. It can make a rat become attracted to the precise thing it was born to fear.

No other brain function of the rodent is impaired. All of its senses are intact, the olfactory bulb required to smell the urine has not suddenly changed. The toxo takes six weeks to go from the gut to the brain, slowly forming cysts on the rat's amygdala. It shrivels up the dendrites of this neural pathway to stop the rodent's fear response to cat urine. It's like someone trying to defuse a bomb with a thousand wires and knowing exactly which one to cut. It secretes an enzyme at the precise moment the rodent senses the urine. The urine activates the production of dopamine, causing the rodent's sexual pathway to come into play.

The rat is now attracted to cat piss.

Imagine a parasite that could go into the human brain, rewire our attraction to bears and make us try and hug a big grizzly. This is beyond the reach of even the most cutting edge technology we have. Sapolsky jokingly points out that this simple parasite knows more about the brain than 25,000 neuroscientists standing on each other's shoulders. This level of humility is admirable but it is also painfully accurate in recognizing how little humans actually know about the human brain. Neuroscientists are like old-world explorers with an incomplete map of the world, blindly sailing to conquest new lands. Just a few hundred years ago these same explorers thought Australia didn't exist and there was a gigantic sea monster in its place. There will be more biological forces that influence our behavior without our control. They are yet to be discovered but the pursuit continues.

Some people might point out that we are not rats and surely our advanced human brains are not susceptible to parasites such as toxo. This is the climax of Sapolsky's work. A growing body of research is examining the effects of toxoplasmosis on humans. It is medical consensus that toxo is a serious threat to the human fetus during pregnancy. But new research has also shown that males in particular become more impulsive after a toxo infection and are 3-4 times more likely to be killed in a motorbike accident that involves reckless speeding.[173] It would appear the parasite is doing the same things in humans as it does in rats. It is rewiring parts of our fear responses and rewarding us for risky behavior. If you are not terrified of the prospect of an unknown parasite changing your way of thinking, the military's interest in toxo should be enough to scare you.

When one considers the behavioral changes this one parasite can exert on people, one must also consider the unknown effects of the multitude of parasites we have no idea about. Parasites which could be controlling us right now. The human brain is one of the most complex structures in the known universe and we are in our infancy of understanding it. In the words of Marvin Minsky, free will is just the internal forces of the brain we don't yet understand.

Sapolsky is not advocating for the criminal justice system to be abolished because people have no control over their actions. No one wants a society with rules that cannot be enforced. Instead he is arguing for recognition that people are not inherently good or evil. There are contributing factors such as blood glucose levels, sleep quality, prenatal environment, concussive head injury and socioeconomic status which have all been shown to impede self-control and affect moral judgment. Society should be less focused on punishment precisely because of these factors. No one thinks that a driver who has a seizure causing them to crash into someone should be punished.[174] Instead, we all agree that such people should not be allowed to drive. Acknowledging that we have less free will than we think doesn't lead to anarchy but to compassion.

Sapolsky is a scientist not a futurist; he doesn't speculate as much as I do. But his research shows us that we aren't in control as much as we think. Be it someone judging another person's character based on the temperature of the glass they are holding, or a person having their life and actions evaluated by a judge who missed lunch. Our moral judgment, self-control and actions are influenced by factors that we don't even realize are in play. Including a potential parasite that is in you right now.

Realizing that free will is more of an illusion than we think can help motivate us to make our society fairer. How can we expect people to exercise enough self-control to get good grades, to get a good job, to be a good citizen when since birth, they have endured inadequate nutrition, sleep deprivation and parental neglect. It's not just about leveling the political playing field; it's about leveling the biological playing field that is secretly influencing things we don't even fully understand. Imagine a world where everyone got access to proper nutrition, good sleep and a caring family. Only then could we compare who chose 'freely' to do right or wrong. But then again, maybe they had a brain tumor pressing against their amygdala like Charles Whitman.

Maybe free will doesn't exist at all.

S. C. GWYNNE

20. THE COMANCHES RULED THE PLAINS

TOPIC: NATIVE INDIANS
GUEST: HISTORIAN / JOURNALIST
PODCAST: #1397
WHERE TO FIND MORE:
EMPIRE OF THE SUMMER MOON (BOOK)

I was on a Greyhound bus from New Orleans to Austin, Texas. For those who have never been on a Greyhound, they are the bus company that every federal prisoner uses with their one free ticket to a destination of their choosing after leaving prison. On this particular day the man sitting next to me had just been released from jail after doing twelve years for armed robbery. He generously offered me whiskey from a brown paper bag, I thanked him but said I was fine. The bus ride was going to be fifteen hours, I strapped in.

It was chaos. Behind me a couple who were clearly on some form of opioid began to cry as they hugged violently, screaming how much "they fucking love each other." In front of me was a man whose bald head was covered completely in tattoos and when he turned to look at me, he had the infamous teardrop inked below his eye. This tattoo is used by many gangs to signify a member's first kill. I was shit scared. Maybe I would need the whiskey after all.

Instead, I put my headphones on and listened to episode #1397 of the Joe Rogan podcast. The guest was someone I had not heard of before.

S.C. Gwynne.

By pure luck, I had picked a historian/journalist who had just finished a book on the Comanche Indians who roamed the plains of Texas and all over the Midwest. The same plains that our Greyhound now traveled across. This was an epic story of the most powerful tribe in American history who shaped the Western frontier. As I looked out of the bus, I saw nothing but flat Texas plains populated with fast-food chains, gas stations and shopping centers. It was a grim sight. There was no natural beauty and the only landmarks were the same franchise every fifteen minutes. Just like farm animals, it seemed the people living in rural Texas had been domesticated by capitalism.

But as I listened to S.C. Gwynne and looked out onto the plains, something else became clear. There was a history that lay in these lands that was so powerful, it can change the way you think. The Comanche Indians ruled the plains, that much is sure, but from this fact there are greater ideas that speak to the limitations of civilization. There is much to learn from the 'uncivilized' as only by comparing our modern-day empires to other cultures, do the strengths and weaknesses of our way of life become glaringly obvious. The story of the Comanche Indians is far more than just a history lesson.

Once upon a time in the Wild West, our story begins. Popularized in film, the Wild West referred to the American frontier, the advancing border of European settlement into hostile land. The frontier saw settlers moving from the Atlantic coast into the unsettled Western States in the 19th century. Such a move was more than dangerous as these settlers were on the outskirts of civilization, entering the home of hostile Native Indians. By this time in history, the Eastern States of America were booming economically and taking the global stage as the world's next empire.

But the West was not yet part of this empire. It was lawless and free yet brutal and unforgiving. The rolling prairies stretched endlessly into the distance with buffalo herds that numbered in the millions. There were mountain ranges, rivers, tundra and forests along with every other type of unadulterated natural landscape. And then there were the lords of the plains, the Comanches. From modern-day Colorado down through Texas, and all the way to the border of Mexico was Comanche territory. This was the most powerful tribe in American history who were considered the greatest warriors on horseback in all of North America. Comanche warriors with arrows could reliably hit an object the size of a doorknob four out of five times while on horseback.[175] They were also buffalo hunting masters, taking down a two-thousand-pound creature with a single arrow. Their culture and entire existence were based around hunting and war. This meant Comanches lived a nomadic life as they would follow the buffalo migration and terrorize other Plains Indians in their path. They were a force like no other.

There was a reason the Spaniards had not been able to push further up into the Americas: the Comanches. After conquering much of South America, the Spaniards tried relentlessly to advance into North America to domesticate and convert local populations to Christianity. History had other plans. They had never encountered such accomplished mounted warriors and after a century and a half of bloody conflict, they more or less conceded defeat to the Comanches.[176]

The next enemy of the Comanches entered their lands blindly, knowing nothing of their existence. The European settlers.

In 1836, Texas was the only place where white settlements met the territory of hostile Plains Indians.[177] It was the bleeding edge of the frontier. Settlers with the promise of land would go where no one else dared, facing unknown and unimaginable dangers. At that time, no one in America really knew who the Comanches were and what they were capable of. It quickly became clear how dangerous life on the frontier was. The Comanches would conduct raids on the settlers where it was custom to take the scalps of men, rape the women and kill babies. There were thousands of these raids that halted the expanding frontier in its tracks. They had entered the plains of the Comanche.

A natural question is why anyone of sound mind would bring their family to settle on a frontier where there was a fair chance they would be tortured and brutally murdered.

> "yet they persisted, bred prolifically, raised their children, farmed their fields and worshipped God, all in a place where almost every waking moment held a mortal threat."[178]

This is how S.C. Gwynne beautifully captures the stubborn, optimistic, foolish, brazen and fierce Calvinist work ethic common among so many of these frontier farming families. It's little wonder the South remains so different from the Northern States when you consider the type of people who first lived on the frontier. They left a legacy that lasts to this day. He goes on to say:

> "They were said to fear God so much that there was no fear left over for anyone or anything else."

It captures the relentlessness of the American empire, a capitalist world built on growth. Everything was always expanding in pursuit of more and more resources to sustain itself. Families would give up everything for the promise of greater fortunes on the edges of the empire. This is the first major contrast to 'uncivilized' native tribes. The Comanche had everything they needed on the plains: buffalo, water and their people. They lived incredibly free lives from all accounts, at least the men did, with multiple sexual partners, ample time to do what they pleased and no taxes to pay. On the other hand, the white settlers lived brutally tough lives as they worked on their land doing backbreaking work, eating rancid meat and adhering to strict puritan moral values. Yet somehow, these settlers were more determined to keep pushing the boundaries of the frontier in the hope of financial gain. Capitalism is a powerful system. So powerful it can make men choose to lead lives of great discomfort for the uncertain promise of eventual comfort. The Plains Indians did not understand this way of life.

One of these frontier families was the Parker family who made their own fort near modern-day Dallas. Their story embodies the horrors of frontier family life. I will not go into too much detail as S.C. Gwynne's incredible book charts the Parker family's grand narrative including their relationship to Comanche war chief, Quanah. But the Parker Fort is one of the most famous stories on the frontier; it's downright unbelievable.

The extended family of about two dozen were tending their crops. Everything was quiet. Out of nowhere, more than a hundred Comanches emerged with a white flag as a sign they were coming peacefully. This was a tactic commonly used by the Plains Indians and was a complete farce. The Parkers knew it too, as some of the women and children fled through the fort's back door. Benjamin Parker went out to meet the Comanches to stall for time. He was surrounded, impaled by their spears and then scalped. After that the

Comanches stormed through the open fort gate, brutally murdering five family members and taking another five captive, most of whom were raped and tormented. The most famous captive was Cynthia Ann Parker, who was eight years old at the time.

She was adopted into the Comanche tribe. This was common practice – the Comanches regularly adopted white, Spanish and other Indian children captured from their raids. Cynthia Ann Parker lived for twenty-five years among the Comanches. She completely forgot English, married a war chief, and had Comanche children of her own. This is remarkable considering the tribe had attacked and killed her family in the Parker Fort Massacre. But what's even more remarkable is that it would happen to her twice. Confederate troops would later kill her husband and many of her tribe, taking her back into Western society once more, a full twenty-five years later. She was a stranger to the very culture she was born in and was utterly miserable. Her religion was that of the Comanches, a form of animism that believed everything in the universe possessed a spirit including plants, trees and rivers. She longed to roam free.

Cynthia Ann Parker's desire to return to the freedom of the plains was articulated best by war chief Ten Bears from the Yamparika tribe. In 1867, U.S. Congress arranged for a peace treaty with the largest congregation of Native Indian chiefs. The chiefs were offered money and resources if they stopped their way of life and lived out their days on reservations, sections of land allotted to them by the government. Ten Bears had this to say:

I DO NOT WANT THEM. I WAS BORN UNDER THE PRAIRIE, WHERE THE WIND BLEW FREE AND THERE WAS NOTHING TO BREAK THE LIGHT OF THE SUN. I WAS BORN WHERE THERE WERE NO ENCLOSURES AND EVERYTHING DREW A FREE BREATH. I WANT TO DIE THERE AND NOT WITHIN WALLS.[179]

Although translated, it is one of the most elegant speeches from what Americans of the time would have thought was a subhuman. It would have made little sense to them back then that a group of people impoverished by their material standards could be content with that way of life. It undermined the belief that only Western civilization knew the way man was meant to live. Civilized.

Only in the 21st century when you look out and see the plains populated with franchise stores and unhappy people, does such a view make complete sense. Joe Rogan, a multi-millionaire, chooses to spend his money on hunting real meat, talking with real people and practicing shooting a bow. The irony that we can only do these things for a living if we have a lot of money shows how wayward civilization can be. We now have to pay for the things that were once free to every human being on the Earth. The Comanches certainly didn't want to give up their freedom for material possessions; they saw the trap.

It's important to realize that the Comanches were capable of heinous acts of violence, violating all of society's codes of conduct. One could argue this is the cost of civilization, peace in exchange for freedom. That's what makes S.C. Gwynne such a good storyteller. He does not attempt to apply a political lens to the facts of history, he simply tells it how it is. Both sides committed treacherous acts of violence. Plains Indians killed other Plains Indians. Whites killed Plains Indians and Plains Indians killed whites. Everyone is guilty in retrospect, not just imperial America, although their later treatment of Indians does render them pretty damn guilty.

Eventually, the buffalo of the plains were killed. It was the usual culprit – capitalism. The Eastern States developed new technology that could make buffalo hide into leather; the result was the price of a hide went up to US$3.50 in 1874.[180] This exorbitant amount made buffalo hunters rich as they set about the extermination of buffalo from the face of the continent. Their numbers dropped from about sixty million in 1500 to a thousand in 1910. Entire towns were established to support the booming buffalo trade as saloons, brothels and sheriffs popped up all over the West.

The Comanche way of life was over.

The rise and fall of the Comanches is a tale far greater than this chapter. It is a story of unchallenged dominance, mustangs, gun powder, Texas Rangers, the Civil War, revolvers, pursuits, massacres and stakeouts. There is still a lot more to discover in the history of the frontier. When you look out onto the Texas prairies that now have McDonalds, Buckies and Walmart, think of the plains that were once ruled by the Comanches.

It turns out the uncivilized had a lot to teach the civilized. They lived lives of unbridled freedom with everything they needed provided by the land. Now the buffalo are gone and fast- food restaurants take their place. It might be easier to get in the car to get a Big Mac but young boys with spears used to ride wild mustangs as they chased their food at high speeds. The exhilaration would be unlike anything we experience in modern-day life. Yet because of our incessant need for economic growth, our culture has given up many of the things that brought us together.

The Greyhound bus arrived in Austin as I looked at the building and shops, I couldn't help but think, was this all worth it?

DR RHONDA PATRICK

21. HUMANS HAVE FORGOTTEN HOW TO EAT

TOPIC: DIET
GUEST: SCIENTIST
PODCAST: #773, #901, #1054, #1474
WHERE TO FIND MORE:
FOUND MY FITNESS (WEBSITE)

I took a class on diet and nutrition at university; it was a topic I was very interested in. My dad was fanatically into the low carb diet and had an Alex Jones-like level of disdain for the food establishment. Although he was a doctor and very well-read on the topic, I still wanted to hear the mainstream opinion. So I arrived in the lecture hall excited to hear what professionals with PHDs in diet and nutrition thought about what we should eat. The first lecture we had, the professor pointed to a graph showing how many carbohydrates Australians eat as a percentage of their diet. She said our carbohydrate intake was too low; we needed to increase it.

This seemed odd. At this point I should probably flag that my professor was overweight, very overweight. I say this not to shame her but rather highlight the irony that at a tertiary level we were receiving dietary advice from someone who, by objective measurements of health, had failed. It was like receiving a lecture on environmental sustainability from an oil baron.

Throughout the course I tried to be as polite as possible, and refraining from such comments, I would raise my hand and ask the lecturer what she thought about intermittent fasting and the science showing refined carbohydrates had negative health impacts.

Eventually I had to have a meeting with the professor because she was not happy with my input. On speaking to her, it became clear she was not reading any journal articles and the slides she used had been in circulation for more than seven years. This professor was teaching students – many of whom would become dieticians themselves – and her advice was to increase our carbohydrate intake? Some of her other claims included sugar is not to blame for diabetes and all types of fats are bad, even the types found in avocados and salmon. Something was wrong.

Thankfully in the age of the internet I could get an education online. Rogan has made a platform for dietary advice where experts can explain their view to millions instead of appearing for two minutes on talk shows making jokes about brussels sprouts making you fart. It's a brave new world of information.

The next guest is none other than Dr Rhonda Patrick, she is a distinguished scientist renowned in the academic field of longevity. She is routinely on the podcast to dispel nutritional myths that many of us, sadly, are taught by the food establishment. Unsurprisingly, as a longevity expert who specializes in diet, Dr Patrick looks young and healthy. Both my professor and Dr Patrick practiced what they preached and it was easy to see whose science on nutrition was not working. How did we get to the point where reputable universities teach us to eat more carbohydrates and we have to turn to a podcast for unbiased dietary advice? How the fuck did we get here?

It's a tale of lies, big business and big pharma.

Our story begins with the now famous food pyramids. These pyramids are supposed to serve as nutritional guides – explaining what the average person is meant to eat. Countries like America, Australia and the U.K. all have similar versions of this government-sanctioned diet advice. On the bottom layer of the pyramid are foods that should make up the bulk of our diet: rice, bread and pasta. These are all carbohydrates. The next layer of the pyramid is vegetables, followed by dairy, meats, poultry, and finally – on the pyramid's apex – we have things like salt and margarine. As you might have noticed, the higher you go in the pyramid, the more you find things that contain fats such as fish, meat and butter.

The general gist of the diet is to eat more carbohydrates and fewer fats. There have been changes over the decades but currently this is what governments and the food establishment encourage their citizens to eat to prevent chronic disease. It sounds reasonable in theory. But as we look closer we will see the shaky ground upon which this pyramid is built.

In the words of my old professor, "we have come a long way in diet but we still have a long way to go."

Have we come a long way? Has the food advice we have been told been effective? We are currently in the midst of the greatest obesity epidemic and chronic disease crisis ever faced by humanity. In the U.S. 40 percent of adults are obese.[181] In Australia 30 percent of adults are obese and an additional 37 percent of adults are overweight. Like our bellies, these statistics keep getting bigger. Since 1980, the number of obese adults has doubled in the U.S. and the number of obese children has tripled.[182] This upward trend is consistent globally. It is known that obesity is a major risk factor for cardiovascular disease, type 2 diabetes and cancer. The obesity epidemic goes hand in hand with the health care burden of chronic disease expected to kill 52 million people per year and cost the global economy US$47 trillion by the year 2030.[183] If we put aside the numbers and think about this in terms of people, someone we know and love will suffer from a chronic disease that causes years of suffering and eventually death. What we eat has a direct impact on obesity and chronic disease. And I think it's safe to say there is something increasingly wrong with what we are eating. The gatekeepers of dietary information are wrong; the food pyramid is collapsing.

The harsh reality is that what we are being told to eat is killing us. But what's worse is that it is the usual culprits behind the misinformation being spread to the public, big industry. In 1970, Luise Light worked with the United States Department of Agriculture (USDA) to update the food pyramid which had been in place since 1956. She was told she was being monitored by the agricultural industry and other heavy hitters in the food business. As part of her recommendations she suggested only two to three servings of refined carbohydrates.[184] The body processes refined carbohydrates like sugar so she was convinced that any more than that would lead to a massive increase in obesity in the general public.

They sent the pyramid back. Without any evidence or reason, USDA wanted six to eleven servings of grain. The pyramid was finalized and it became unlawful for schools and food stamp programs to provide less than this amount of servings. That year those changes netted US$350 million to the American wheat industry – and netted the American public an obesity epidemic decades later. But how does the food industry get away with this? The *Dietary Guidelines for Americans* is written by a panel where 38 percent of proposed members had no diet or nutrition experience.[185] Instead, the panel is staffed with people with ties to industry to ensure their interests are looked after. The only obesity expert on the panel in 2015 worked for Nestlé. So the people providing dietary advice and food pyramids are also tied to the food that makes people unhealthy in the first place. This conflict of interest leads to the public being told whatever is necessary to keep consuming the products they sell, even if they cause irreparable harm.

What should we eat? How do we eat in our best interests and not those of big business? It seems like such a simple question yet we are confronted with terminology such as ketosis, macronutrients, paleo, veganism, epigenetics and gut microbes. The minefield of confusing terms, diets and marketing can make picking what to eat harder than picking a spouse.

Thankfully, Dr Rhonda Patrick provides principles to help answer this question. It's important to recognize that she does not claim to have all the answers; nutrition is far too complex a field with many different foods suited to different people. One of the first principles that Dr Patrick advocates is to customize your diet based on your genes. This is called nutrigenomics. You might have a certain DNA mutation that makes some foods unfavorable. For example, the PPAR alpha gene can affect fatty metabolism and is particularly good to know if you are embarking on a high-fat diet. What might cause weight loss for one person might result in nutritional deficiencies for another. It's the same reason some people can eat only cheeseburgers and stay skinny while others get fat from eating a single Cheeto. Thankfully there are now affordable commercial gene profiling companies who can help you pick the best diet based on your genome. This is technology that has never been available before and it will change the way we eat.

For those who can't afford this, there are principles that will benefit most people for no extra cost. The first principle that Dr Patrick advocates is to avoid refined sugars and grains (carbohydrates). People in the establishment such as my old professor would disagree with this, but the evidence does not support them, big industry does. There are several studies on her website, *Found my Fitness* but the most telling is the following: a meta-analysis comparing a low carbohydrate diet to a low-fat diet found that the low carbohydrate diet led to greater weight loss.[186] How could a low-fat diet possibly not be good for losing fat? It sounds like saying drinking less water won't make you thirsty. Unlike water however, there are different types of fat and some are essential for health while others are harmful. Fats found in avocado, milk, meat, butter and fish are actually an important part of the diet. Fats found in pies, pizzas and cakes are – unsurprisingly –not good for you.

In the past there has been no distinction between 'good' and 'bad' fats, and the reason why dates back to 1976 when the flawed cholesterol hypothesis captured the public's attention. When tight yoga pants, infomercials, and cheesy workouts were at their prime, the public was told a high-fat diet leads to higher cholesterol, leading to heart attacks. Shoppers quickly swapped out regular products for their 'low-fat' counterparts and avoided foods such as eggs, red meat and butter. These myths continue today and somehow my professor had still not updated her lecture slides from 2013. In 2015 even the USDA themselves publicly admitted this flawed hypothesis was not correct.[187] Eggs and shellfish do not lead to heart attacks because they increase cholesterol. The public was once again told the wrong thing.

All the misinformation might seem disheartening. How are you meant to pick the right things to eat when big industry does everything they can to confuse you? Both Rogan and Dr Patrick have a simple answer.

Eat food that you could find outside.

Plants that grow in the ground and animals that roam the land. You won't find pasta or pies resting atop a tree, so humans are not optimized to eat them. For all science's advancements in nutrition, they are really a rediscovery of what humans in the past already knew. The big food industry has only been around for about 100 years; the agricultural industry has been around for 10,000 years but homo sapiens have been around for more than 200,000 years. Early humans had to find food wherever they could, eating every conceivable plant and shrub and every type of animal from lobsters to rats, elephants to elk. Our bodies evolved to eat these unprocessed foods. To suggest that hunter-gathers should not have eaten salmon and avocado because they are high in saturated fats or not eaten meat because it is 'correlated' with cancer is absurd. It's absurd because tribes, even ones with diets high in meat had virtually no chronic disease. Ethnographic evidence, where modern doctors examine these tribes disconnected from modern life, shows almost no cases of hypertension, heart disease, gout or dementia and memory loss.[188] Infectious disease and broken limbs were rife but chronic disease was exceedingly rare. An example is the Tokelauan people whose diet consisted of fish, coconuts and breadfruit. No cases of obesity were observed, but when the Tokelauan people began to import foods from the modern world such as sugar and wheat, chronic disease reared its ugly head. Big industry had arrived.

Refined carbohydrates and sugar are the predominant forces behind the global obesity epidemic.

There is another problem. Fats, carbohydrates and proteins are macronutrients, but minerals and vitamins are also essential for humans. These are called micronutrients. While people are consuming more and more food, they consume less and less of these vital micronutrients. It is like running your car on diesel mixed with sewage water, your tank might be full but the car is still fucked. Dr Patrick's research looks at how these nutritional deficiencies are causing a host of problems for people. Not getting enough vitamin D is linked to depression, a lack of vitamin C weakens the immune system and the list goes on. In America, 42 percent of people have vitamin D deficiencies. When one thinks about the mental health epidemic ravaging the Western world, one can't help but think how much of this suffering would be eased from people receiving adequate micronutrients. Back to our car running on diesel with sewage water – we wouldn't medicate the car with a new exhaust, we would just change the fuel.

The third principle Dr Patrick advocates is the use of smoothies to get micronutrients and the proper fuel for your body to function. By simply blending a range of particular vegetables and fruit you get all the micronutrients you need. Her science-based recipes can be found on her website.

They say the Egyptian pyramids were built by the slaves of pharaohs. It seems coincidental that the people who built the nutritional pyramids of recent history were also enslaved, albeit by a different master – big industry. In the age of information, we no longer have to listen to overweight professors or panels of people paid for by food companies. The Joe Rogan podcast has allowed leading experts with no invested interest other than improving their followers' health and wellness to broadcast diet advice to the masses. Now it is time to reclaim food from the people poisoning us with lies.

It's time to eat real food.

Here is a list of key takeaways from Dr Rhonda Patrick's work:

- Avoid most refined sugars and grains. She advocates for a diet of vegetables, fruit, meat and fish.
- Use smoothies to get a range of micronutrients that most Americans are deficient in.
- Use nutrigenomics to see what type of foods are best for your individual body. Different foods are better for different people.
- Incorporate some form of fasting into your diet. Dr Rhonda Patrick uses intermittent fasting where she only eats for ten hours of the day and fasts for the other fourteen hours. This usually means not eating breakfast.

JOHANN HARI

22. DEPRESSION IS NOT JUST A CHEMICAL IMBALANCE

TOPIC: MENTAL HEALTH
GUEST: JOURNALIST
PODCAST: #1077, #1250
WHERE TO FIND MORE:
LOST CONNECTIONS (BOOK)

The Aokigahara forest sits at the base of Mount Fuji. The forest grows on top of a hardened layer of lava left by centuries-old volcanic eruptions. Many often get lost among its sprawling trees and dense fauna. Sadly, the Aokigahara forest is known by another name. It is Japan's infamous suicide forest. Bodies are found hanging throughout the forest as hundreds come to the spot each year to take their lives. There is a spike in deaths just after the fiscal year when companies must report their financial results. It is a tragic example of two worlds colliding. The suffering of modern existence being showcased in the natural world.

I will not pretend I learned about this forest from something pretentious like a book or a haiku. I found it on a YouTube video. It had a long-lasting impact on me and made me think seriously about modern life's shortfalls. What was driving people in countries all over the world to this point? More confusingly, what was responsible for the increase in suicides in Western countries. Somehow in countries where people have more we are made to feel less. This paradox confused me for some time. Poor mental health is a growing epidemic in some of the most affluent countries such as the United States, the

United Kingdom and Australia. Millions wake up in an unbearable state of depression and anxiety each day. It seems to be one of the greatest challenges the modern world faces and most of us don't even know where to begin to solve it. Antidepressants? A motivational TED talk? Buying a new car?

Then I listened to Johann Hari on the podcast. I sat in a trance as three hours felt like a second. I then purchased his book *Lost Connections* and the twelve hours of reading felt like a few minutes. His main idea is this: antidepressants are not the best solution to depression. Instead the solution can be found in our environment. This is undoubtedly one of the most controversial ideas in the book. The type of idea that requires an obligatory acknowledgment that nothing you read here is to be taken as medical advice. I have always thought that when someone prefaces their medical opinion in that way, it is a giant red flag and they are not to be trusted. It's like saying listen to my advice but don't actually take it as advice because I don't know. That's not the case in this instance. Such a legal warning is necessary when you realize the power of the opponents Hari is up against. The pharmaceutical industry.

A fake narrative about depression and anxiety has been sold to the general public. People were told they were depressed or anxious due to a chemical imbalance in their brains. They had low levels of serotonin and needed to return their brains to normal. The solution was antidepressants. The 1990s saw the exponential rise of Prozac, an antidepressant administered to millions of people from teenagers to housewives to executives and workers worldwide. It promised to restore the chemical equilibrium of happiness. All that was needed was to swallow a pill. This narrative was one that I was familiar with having studied mental health at a university – albeit at a basic level.

Before we go further we must understand why this fake narrative permeates our culture. At university our professors teach us that for medication to be sold in America it must be approved by the Food Drug Administration (FDA). The FDA will approve a drug to the public if it shows a significant positive effect compared to a placebo in two clinical trials. A clinical trial in its simplest form involves a treatment group and a control group. The treatment group gets the active drug and the control group gets a placebo. The placebo is something that looks identical to the actual drug but contains no active ingredient. It's like the 'magic potion' that Ronald Weasley drinks in Harry Potter, causing him to have the best Quidditch game of his life. Ron later finds out the magic potion was water and it was the belief that he drank magic that made him perform so well. This is the placebo effect and it turns out our beliefs and expectations have an incredible capacity to cause actual biological change.

So how is it possible that antidepressants aren't effective if they must go through this rigorous scientific process? The pharmaceutical industry is rigging the trials, alleges Johann Hari. This claim instinctively made me skeptical and question whether I was going down the rabbit hole of some Eddie Bravo-style conspiracy theory so I googled Johann Hari and did some snooping. It turns out he has a somewhat questionable character and made an exodus from mainstream journalism due to plagiarizing his colleagues' work. This was worrying and maybe it was just an unfounded conspiracy against big pharma coming from a disgraced tin foil hat journalist. Then I read Irving Kirsch's scientific reports, who Hari mentioned in his book. Johann Hari was correct. The pharmaceutical industry was deceiving the masses.

Those clinical trials are being run by pharmaceutical companies who do not have to publish their results to the public.[189] They only have to release the two successful trials they obtain for the antidepressants to be approved. This is a major loophole as they can run as many trials as they like until two trials show any positive effect. This means the countless failed trials where the drugs were shown to be ineffective are not released to the public. That was the case until Irving used the Freedom of Information Act to request the FDA provide the datasets of all the unpublished trials for a meta-analysis.

The results undermine a multi-billion-dollar industry whose deception probably affects people you know. The drugs have little if any chemical effect in helping treat depression. More than half of the trials showed that antidepressants had no more effect than the placebo, the pill with nothing in it. Even more shockingly, 82 percent of the response to antidepressants was a response to the placebo.

This needs to be put into perspective to show how insignificant the chemical effect actually is. The Hamilton Depression Rating Scale (HAM-D) is used to measure people's depression on a scale of 0-53. The difference between the drug and the placebo on this scale is only 1.8.[190] To put that into perspective, changing sleep patterns can cause a six-point change in someone's HAM-D. A change of less than three is regarded as clinically insignificant by health authorities in the United Kingdom. This basically means if not for the placebo effect, the drug would be of no use to a mental health clinician. While there might be a small statistical effect, it has virtually no observable effect in the real world. Some will push back against Hari here and say that absolutely anything that could help someone's depression should be used.

Why does it matter if people use antidepressants in the same way as a placebo? As long it makes them feel better then that's all that's important? Right? This would be true were it not for the documented side effects of these drugs. Placebos are inert. Antidepressants have chemicals that affect multiple other human functions. They can cause obesity, sexual dysfunction and there is even some evidence showing an increased risk of suicidal thoughts.[191] A drug made to help prevent suicide may actually increase the likelihood of suicide in some patients. This is absurd.

The narrative that depression is just a chemical imbalance in someone's brain that can be solved by simply swallowing a pill is wrong. Johann Hari shares his own battle with depression in his book and expresses genuine empathy for those going through a similar struggle. Importantly he does acknowledge that for a select few with severe depression, these drugs may be useful. But by and large they are not the answer. He is not being provocative for attention but instead to send a message that people are not born broken. Depression is not something caused by chemicals in your brain but by various factors in your life. It is a signal – just like pain – that your needs as a human being are not addressed. In the words of Hari, "You aren't a machine with broken parts. You are an animal whose needs are not being met."[192]

This might seem like pseudo-psychology designed to warm your heart, but credible scientific evidence supports this view. But before we look at Hari's arguments, it helps to consider the absurdity of the situation our species now find ourselves in.

Rogan has spent many hours addressing this: we are a species that evolved on the savannahs of Africa, and for almost all of human evolution we lived in intensely interconnected tribes that relied on each other for survival. There was no existential angst in a world where everyone's clear purpose was getting food to eat, water to drink and avoiding predators. The food we consumed was, by definition, natural – preservatives, added sugar and food dyes were non-existent. We spent all our time in the natural world attuned to the change of seasons as the summer Sun became the autumn wind. We were constantly moving as our bodies were the only form of transport we had. Since the agricultural revolution humans no longer live like this. The majority of people in the West now find themselves at office desks with no windows to know if it is day or night. People wear suits and answer to a boss in an autocratic chain of command where the only decision they can make is what they get from the vending machine. There is no need to exercise or eat natural food as fast-food chains and couches are infinitely more appealing. To top it all off, most people don't even know their neighbor as they live in increasing isolation despite this being the most populous time in human history.

Although Hari refrains from such prose it helps to reflect his central idea. It is the disconnection from the way we were made to live which causes depression. People need community, meaningful work, a sense of respect, meaningful values and connection to nature to feel healthy.[193] Hari skillfully weaves a narrative of anecdotal and scientific evidence showing how changing these factors can reduce depression.[194] One of the most profound pieces of evidence presented in the book comes from a study done by Ernest Moore on inmates at the state prison of Southern Michigan. The prison was constructed such that half the building faced tranquil countryside and the other half faced bleak brick walls. He examined the medical records of the two groups of prisoners whose cells faced either the countryside or the brick walls. Remarkably the group who could see the natural world was 24 percent less likely to get physically or mentally unwell.

One thing notably absent from Hari's book and his discussion on the podcast, is how effective diet and exercise can be in reducing depression. It seems odd that they weren't touched on as they exemplify the modern world's disconnection from our evolutionary past. A study in 2017 was one of the first to show dietary intervention could cause a reduction in depression.[195] The most fascinating part of the study is that the treatment group only received nutritional consulting sessions with a dietician. There was no forced change in diet. The control group received a social support session for the same length of time as the diet session. Incredibly, it was more effective to talk to someone who could help you change your diet than it was to talk to someone just to receive general support.

For those who are deeply depressed, it's pretty insulting to say quit your job, become a hiking instructor and eat asparagus. That is why depression is so deadly. It's a negative spiral where the motivation needed to build up positive habits to make people feel better is simply not there. Depression is a problem to be solved collectively not individually. Everyone is responsible. Instead of focusing only on our immediate families' wellbeing, we need to extend our concern to the wellbeing of communities. In every suburb there is an old man or woman who has not spoken to anyone for weeks, longing to say hello to someone.

People in positions of power need to give workers more responsibility and think about how they can make their work environments more positive places to be. The leadership style of a single manager could be causing many to have a miserable existence.[196] I have worked in a call center job where my boss told me that I had to go home because I was wearing slides. Because the customers can see my feet? The soul-crushing bureaucracy of mid-level managers probably amounts for a great deal of people's unhappiness in the world. Diet, exercise and mindfulness need to be a focus of education. Without giving schoolchildren the tools to address their mental health, society is effectively sending them into a battle armed only with a pool noodle.

Depression needs to stop being an isolated personal battle treated by pills, and instead become a collective responsibility to be solved by all of us. For all the advancements in science, they seem only to affirm things we already knew. People need a sense of community, purpose and a healthy lifestyle to be happy. But when someone is in the depths of despair they need a helping hand from those around them to pull them out. That hand needs to come from society not the pharmaceutical industry.

DAVID SINCLAIR

23. AGING CAN BE STOPPED

TOPIC: LONGEVITY
GUEST: SCIENTIST
PODCAST: #1234, #1349
WHERE TO FIND MORE: LIFESPAN (BOOK)

David Sinclair sits opposite Joe Rogan in the studio. The man looks like he is thirty.

"How old are you?" asks Rogan.
"Fifty," David replies.

It is of little surprise when you find out his occupation is leading a Harvard laboratory focused on stopping aging. It is like a researcher of LSD coming to the studio high. Sinclair is clearly high on his own supply, which happens to be molecules that might extend human life. It is safe to say the world's leading geneticist knows something that most people don't. Does he hold the keys to the eternal fountain of youth? Through his multiple podcast appearances and book *Lifespan*, he just might have the answer. It just might be possible for humans to live substantially longer than we were meant to. Maybe even forever.

Aging is not considered a disease by governments. Everyone assumes it's just a fact of life – grey hair and asking the same question three times over. There seems to be little point in trying to stop an inevitable fact of life, death.

Everyone ages and then dies. Instead, the medical field solves specific problems one by one. The system classifies specific pathologies and then addresses them in isolation. Heart attacks. Strokes. Cancers.

If the cure to all cancers was discovered how much longer do you think humans would live for on average? Twenty years? Ten years? The answer is 2.1 more years of life.[197] Take a moment to process how minuscule an outcome this is for such a huge achievement. Stop all cancers and humans only live for 2.1 more years on average. And that doesn't even factor in the quality of those extra years of human life. Western medicine is hell bent on extending lifespan with little regard to individuals' healthspan. There is an important difference. Lifespan is the number of years you live for and healthspan is how many years of good health you live for. Few will disagree that extending older individuals' lives is of little value if their existence is consumed by pain and slow decline as they spend their last decade of life trapped in a hospital ward. Put bluntly, what is the point?

There is a reason that stopping all cancers has such little effect on increasing the quality and length of human life. When people enter the last few decades of their life, as doctors address one problem, another problem arises. To illustrate this point, consider that smoking causes a fivefold increase in the chances of having certain cancers.[198] This is a lot. However, being fifty years old increases your chances a hundredfold. It would appear it is far more dangerous to be middle-aged than it is to smoke. Being seventy increases your chances by a thousandfold. That's just cancer. As you approach eighty, there is an army of diseases ready to take you down. People who are eighty-five years old can on average expect to be diagnosed with four different diseases.[199] The current medical approach could be likened to plugging each individual hole in a sinking ship with a piece of gum. Not to belittle the important research that is being done but unless there is a unified approach to why these diseases are occurring in the first place, the multi-billion-dollar quest to end cancer won't end the suffering of millions of old people – they'll just be diagnosed with something else the next day.

What if the underlying disease is aging itself?

Instead of plugging each hole, Sinclair proposes it might be possible to build a better ship. By combating age as a disease, all the subsidiary diseases – that almost all of us will likely die from, are addressed. Delaying aging delays death from painful and often debilitating diseases which eventually deprive us of our very own identity. Most people are afraid of extending life because they don't want to live as a shadow of their younger selves. What if we could live past eighty feeling like we were twenty and then die a dignified death. And why might our descendants not have to die at all?

But first, why do we die? Is it in our DNA? No, it's not. There is no gene for death. Sinclair's revolutionary *Informational Theory of Aging* is the most cutting-edge scientific explanation for why humans age. And why they might not have to. The theory is that aging occurs because of a loss of epigenetic information. Not even twenty years ago could you get such a concise answer for why we age. Importantly, it explains telomere lengths, mitochondrial dysfunction and all the other hallmarks of aging in one unified theory. I will now attempt to condense a year's worth of university biology and a book's worth of theoretical information into a simple analogy to explain why we die and how we can exploit it. If you want more than just a superficial understanding, the book is an exceptional resource.

Our DNA is a blueprint for every cell in our body. It lays out the instructions for how our bodies should be put together. Until very recently no one really knew how we aged. Some people thought it might be because our DNA mutates. It turns out that our DNA can remain intact for tens of thousands of years. When we die, our blueprints still exist – buried under the ground like a map to the treasure chest of life.

So why do we die if our DNA could technically live forever? Think of the differences between identical twins. Their DNA is 100 percent the same. They share the same blueprint. The reason that one might get lung cancer and the other does not is because of the epigenome. All our DNA is called our genome. The collection of genes that we are born with. The epigenome is how the genome is regulated. It switches genes 'on' and 'off' at different times. Sinclair's breakthrough theory suggests that it is the loss of epigenetic information that causes aging. By finally understanding this process, humans might be able to change the entire course of the species.

The rodent world will never be the same. Sinclair's laboratory has extended the life of mice by radically slowing aging.[200] For the first time in history, a species has fooled the clock of the universe and changed an organism's age.

How did they do it?

Magic?

Basketball might offer a better explanation than magic. Think of the players on a basketball team as different genes. Each player is one gene. Now think of the coach as the epigenome, he tells the player when to play offense and when to play defense. We age because the coach starts giving us the wrong instructions. He tells the players to play defense when they have the ball. They do the wrong thing and there is a turnover. This happens in cells when a loss of epigenetic information causes genes to be silenced or activated when they shouldn't be. Cells lose their correct function and do the wrong thing. For example, a cell that should be an optic nerve in our eye loses its function because of epigenetic noise. The coach has given it the wrong instructions and now the cell in our eye is not being an optic nerve. Hence our vision gets worse as we grow older.

But what causes the coach to give the wrong instructions? Or more importantly how is the epigenetic information being lost. The answer to this might be the key to a longer life. Let's return to the basketball analogy. Assume that the players on the field have no idea what to do unless the coach tells them. On the bench of the basketball team are some very smart nerds. They aren't the best players but their knowledge of basketball is impeccable. They are truly master tacticians. So much so that they tell the coach all the strategy he needs to know. Were it not for them, the coach would have no idea what to tell the players on the field. The players would be useless. Occasionally though, a player on the field gets injured. A nerd must sub on for them while the injured player recovers. There are still enough nerds telling the coach how to play the game. But another player gets injured. And another. Eventually all the nerds are on the court and all the jocks are on the bench. The coach has no idea what to do. Chaos ensues. The nerds are running around playing random positions they should not be in. Playing defense when they should be playing offense. They lose the game.

This is how you die from aging. Your biology isn't as basic as nerds and jocks but this is roughly how the process works.

If you recall, all players in the game are your genomes and the coach is the epigenome. The nerds on the bench are a very special type of gene. They are called the sirtuin genes or longevity genes. They are the basis of an ancient survival circuit which is believed to be in every living organism. When there is DNA damage – the player getting injured – the sirtuin stops its job of telling the coach what to do and goes on the field. The nerd comes back to the bench when the player is healed. In scientific language, the sirtuin genes have two important functions. They regulate epigenetic information and are involved in DNA repair. When there is too much damage to DNA, they neglect their role of regulating vital epigenetic information. As a result, cells lose their function as they are activated and silenced at the wrong time, causing cell senescence, aging. In sporting terms, if too many players are getting injured, the nerds have to sub on. If too many go on, then the coach has no idea how to direct the players. He tells the nerds to play offense when they should be playing defense. They play horribly and lose. We die.

Now for the revolutionary part. It turns out that while much of modern medicine has extended our lifespan, our modern habits have not. Our bodies are desperately trying to stay in homeostasis. This just means the body will always try to stay in equilibrium. It wants to be the same temperature, eat food regularly and do as little exercise as possible. This is deadly. It signals to our body that times are good and our ancient survival circuit switches off. It's like the players on the bench all stuffing their faces with food and drink because they don't think they will go on the court. They inevitably will have to but when they do they will be hopelessly unprepared. The nerds need to go on every now and then to keep developing their skills on the court. Just not too much that they are on all the time. While chronic stress can reduce life and accelerate aging, just the right amount of stress is the key to extended life. This is the holy grail of longevity advice.

Sinclair and others in the field of aging have all confirmed that activation of our ancient survival circuit is vital for longevity. Controlled amounts of bodily stress activate the sirtuin genes which make our bodies utilize all of its mechanisms to survive and live longer. It makes sense from an evolutionary point of view. If times are good, we eat and reproduce, our job is done. There is little need from evolution's perspective for keeping humans around. But when times are tough, food is scarce, and only those that can bunker down and survive will live long enough to reproduce. This activates our survival circuit.

Here is a list of exactly how you can exploit this ancient survival network in your own life:

- Eat less (Calorie reduction has been shown to increase lifespan in humans and monkeys)[201]

- Intermittent fasting (Animal studies show benefit for cellular health with recent human studies seeming to support this)[202]
- Exercise (Ten minutes of moderate exercise a day is shown to add years to human life)[203]
- Sauna (Frequency of sauna use appears to be correlated to risk of all-cause mortality. Specifically, increased use of sauna directly correlates with decreased rates of all-cause mortality)[204]
- Being cold (Animal studies show that rats exposed to cold temperatures for a few hours a day reduce rates of diabetes, obesity and Alzheimer's disease)[205]

All of these actions, with scientific evidence, involve pushing your body out of its homeostatic point to activate the survival circuit, thus living a longer and healthier life. The right amount of stress is good. It should be noted that some of these have only been correlated with longer life and are yet to be shown as the causal reason. This isn't surprising as two decades ago the cause of aging was unknown, let alone how to stop it.

There are molecules that can mimic the effect of these strategies. Although testing these molecules on humans has just begun, they have been proven in different animals to extend life by activating this ancient survival circuit that we all share. The fountain of youth is just a few years away. These molecules work by either increasing the activity of the sirtuin genes or making them more effective. The following is not medical advice and is instead the regime David Sinclair follows. The research is promising although not conclusive, so the advice is not to take these compounds right now. That being said, Sinclair takes the following:

- 1 gram of resveratrol (Countless animal studies have shown that resveratrol can extend life. However, scientists are still trying to find ways for humans to absorb it as it is not very soluble)[206]
- 1 gram of nicotinamide mononucleotide (NMN)
- 0.5 gram of metformin (Human studies have shown metformin reduces your biological age by two years. The drug is used to treat diabetes but might be beneficial to all humans for its anti-aging properties)[207]

Some studies have shown resveratrol and metformin can offset the benefits of exercise.[208] Sinclair cycles between them, exercising three days a week then taking these molecules on the other days. Although it's early days, times are changing. The chances are the above chemicals or their undiscovered cousins will be responsible for making you live longer than any human before you.

An anti-aging revolution has begun.

STEVEN KOTLER

24. CONSCIOUSNESS CAN BE HACKED

TOPIC: BIOHACKING
GUEST: JOURNALIST
PODCAST: #873
WHERE TO FIND MORE: STEALING FIRE (BOOK)

The Terminator is an invincible cyborg. Covered in organic human skin, it has a body supplemented with elite biomechatronic parts. Capable of withstanding the direct impact from bullets, and able to regenerate severed limbs, the Terminator is a future soldier that would be almost unstoppable.

It's reassuring to look at photos of the Terminator now, and specifically, the actor who played this never-aging cyborg, Arnold Schwarzenegger. The Terminator has aged, with grey hair and wrinkled skin. A comforting reminder that The Terminator is just a movie and hybrid humans capable of the impossible do not exist.

Well, not yet.

Science fiction movies such as The Terminator are often scary harbingers of what is to come. Many humans currently have prosthetic limbs which can be controlled by their brain; an artificial bionic leg for example is controlled by our own consciousness and, although far from regenerating lost limbs, the future is here.

There is a group of rebels who are fixated on pushing the boundaries of what is currently possible. On peering into the future and stealing technologies for the present.

They are called biohackers and their aim is to hack the hardwiring of our consciousness to optimize human performance. The field of biohacking is in its infancy but is already experiencing an explosion of interest from anyone focused on elite performance. There are endurance athletes, billionaires, U.S. Navy SEALs, musicians and writers all set on pushing the frontiers of the human mind.

To the uninitiated, the practices they use might seem excessive, but a growing body of science is showing they are effective. Some would prefer to go about their day to day lives without entering the world of biohacking but for those curious about testing human mental potential, an underground world awaits.

A man who has switched on the light in the once dark underground of biohacking is Steven Kotler. The New York Times bestselling author, award-winning journalist and one of the world's leading experts on high performance is fairly adept in pushing mental boundaries. Rogan invited him on the podcast after reading his book, *Stealing Fire,* as the comedian said it provided him with the scientific explanation for how his creative process worked. Kotler had put words to a once indescribable process, creativity. But his ideas are not limited to creativity – by explaining the science of consciousness, we can then exploit it for our benefit, in whatever domain we like.

Before we unpack the secrets to accessing our maximum potential, let's see who Kotler has helped achieve maximum performance. To put it bluntly, does he actually get results or is he just another motivational speaker?

If the U.S. Navy SEALs are the tip of the spear for elite forces, then SEAL Team Six is the one atom at the tip of that tip. SEAL Team Six are the most highly trained and expensive group of soldiers to ever walk the Earth. It costs around US$85 million a year to keep them combat-ready due to the special equipment and the cost of their advanced training.[209] They are the team responsible for killing Osama Bin Laden and take on only the highest profile missions. They are elite. Any possible way they can manufacture an advantage on the battlefield they will, especially if it's a mental advantage. Inspired by Kotler's work, they invited him to their training facility in Norfolk, Virginia to examine their 'Mind Gym.'[210]

The 'Mind Gym' is an example of biohacking being utilized to accelerate learning. The unconventional gym consists of sensory deprivation tanks, biometric devices and EEG brain monitors. Through these technologies, the SEALs have been able to cut the time to learn a language from six months to just six weeks.[211] Through hacking consciousness team members can deploy with a remarkable mental edge.

Biohacking is not only being used in warfare, but also in the arts. Creatives are always searching for a way to access a deeper reservoir of ideas – Joe Rogan being one of them. The biggest adopters of biohacking however, come from Silicon Valley. The tech industry is obsessed with optimizing the human brain to solve complex problems that our monkey brains are not equipped to answer. Anyone who wants to push the boundaries in their specialty – from war to art to business – can benefit from accessing more brainpower.

So what is biohacking and how does one hack consciousness? Biohacking is basically a systems-thinking approach to our own biology. Unlike self-help books that rely on motivational words to help the individual, biohacking utilizes science and self-experimentation to maximize the power of our body and minds.

This might all sound pretty up in the air so I will provide a concrete example of what biohackers focus on. They experiment with diet, intermittent fasting, sunlight exposure, temperate regulation, sleep gadgets and nootropics to test their effect on mood, productivity and creativity. Science provides clues for what may work and then they test it on themselves generally using biometrics – the technical term for measuring things in the human body. This can include measuring blood glucose levels, using special devices to monitor sleep levels and taking advantage of blood tests and other commercially available gene profiling companies. As they are the guinea pigs in their own experiments, a biohacker might try a new supplement such as magnesium and monitor their health markers to see if there is an improvement e.g. an increase in sleep quality. If there is, then they will integrate this practice into their life. It might sound extreme but it's a community of people pushing some fairly extreme boundaries. But there is a simple biohack that everyone can access with very minimal effort. How?

Before Kotler knew the answer to that question he studied the top performers in every field from extreme adventure sports to music to business. In interviewing hundreds of these high achievers he noticed a pattern. They all described a similar state of mind when they were in the zone, a similar state of consciousness. This was unusual. Why would someone in a wingsuit flying through a tiny hole in a rock face report the same thing as a composer writing music on a beach?

Then he understood why. High performance people all seemed to be accessing the same altered mental state. One that everyone could access but very rarely used.

The flow state.

The flow state is defined as an, "optimal state of consciousness where we feel our best and perform our best" commonly referred to as being 'in the zone'.[212] The definition of flow state provided by Kotler is too general to gain anything useful; it's more easily explainable through example. You have been in the flow state at least once in your life. It is a state of consciousness where any sense of self or time vanishes. Your focus is so sharp that you lose track of time and the existential worries that fill our waking existence. You might not have experienced flow state in an office but perhaps while hunting, fishing or even walking. Everyone has different activities that activate different levels of being in the flow state. The one thing in common is that performance skyrockets when this state of mind is accessed.

Let's unpack the science of flow state as only then can we hack consciousness and join the leagues of biohackers around the world. Normal consciousness needs no introduction. Most of us spend the majority of our life in this range. What neuroscience reveals about this default mode of consciousness is a predictable and consistent signature of brain activity across virtually all people. The prefrontal cortex is particularly active, brainwaves are in the high-frequency beta range and particular stress chemicals such as cortisol and norepinephrine are present in the brain.[213]

The most interesting part of normal consciousness is the activity of the prefrontal cortex. This is the most recently evolved part of the human brain. Both children and monkeys have significantly smaller prefrontal cortices than an adult human. The prefrontal cortex is responsible for humans being able to delay gratification, use complex reasoning, plan for the future and, most importantly, it gives us a heightened sense of self-awareness.[214] All the things you would probably associate with being an adult. Without this part of the brain becoming so developed in adult humans, we would never have had the ability to wield tools, create civilizations and make memes. The prefrontal cortex has helped make humans the top of the food chain.

Although the cost of the prefrontal cortex has been great. In the words of Kotler:

> "No one built an off switch for the potent self-awareness that made it all possible."[215]

This is the reason that you have a voice inside your head. An egotistical prick who is engaged in a constant internal monologue. Telling you what you are good and bad at, what you can and can't do. The inability to disconnect from this self-chatter and the level of self-criticism it engages in is a source of great depression and anxiety for humans all around the world. We simply can't get the voice in our head to shut the fuck up. I think the Buddhists put it best with, "a wandering mind is an unhappy mind."

Elite performers find a way to switch this voice off when doing what they do best. Their minds are not wondering; they have laser-sharp focus. The flow state offers an escape from normal consciousness, with performance thriving in this alternate state of mind. Being in the flow state also has some classic signatures of brain activity that make it a measurable scientific phenomenon. Brainwaves slow from agitated beta waves to calmer alpha waves. The cocktail of chemicals in the brain also shifts to include more neurotransmitters associated with pleasure such as dopamine and norepinephrine, to eventually releasing endorphins. Most importantly, there is decreased activity of the prefrontal cortex. The inner voice is silenced. This experience is why when you are in the zone you will lose track of time, your worries fade away and it will all feel remarkably effortless. This is called transient hypofrontality – the name for when activity in your prefrontal cortex is reduced. The flow state is liberation, from yourself. And it's highly effective. Spending more time in this state has been shown to dramatically increase creativity.[216] This is because the neurotransmitters activated during flow state encourage the brain to make neural connections that the brain does not normally permit. Your brain combines ideas it would be too scared to try if your inner voice was active.

So how do you achieve flow state and hack your consciousness? There are multiple ways. Kotler highlights that humans are willing to spend a lot of money to get out of their minds. In fact, he puts the altered states economy at US$4 trillion.[217] This is how much humans are willing to spend to get out of their normal way of consciousness – from illicit drugs, legal drugs, EDM, social media or going to the movies. Now I somewhat question his calculation as it is a pretty hard thing to quantify, and including things like social media is a bit questionable. But people undoubtedly enjoy escaping their internal monologue and are willing to pay to silence their inner voice.

Not all ways of achieving flow state are equal. There are traditional methods with well documented efficacy. These ancient methods of reaching flow state include singing, dancing, chanting and meditation. More recently, a range of drugs – psychedelics – have enabled people to achieve a state of mind similar to that observed in flow state. Refer back to Michael Pollan's chapter for how psychedelics can expand consciousness.

Both the ancient and relatively new activities have been shown to cause transient hypofrontality, the flow state. While some are more harmful than others, the more you practice silencing your prefrontal cortex, the better you become at it. Mckinsey & Company, one of the top management consultancy firms in the world, states the average worker spends only 5 percent of their day to day work lives in flow state. They predict that if this was increased to just 15 percent there would be a doubling in overall productivity.[218]

The flow state is essential.

Now for a simple biohack. You can do some easy things in your everyday life to access the flow state – this altered state of consciousness which is scientifically proven to improve productivity. Stop distractions. This sounds eerily like a self-help mantra so I have attached my own condensed list of how to try and achieve the flow state using biohacking.

- Use noise-canceling headphones and play 'alpha wave' music. This music mimics the frequency of your brain waves in flow state. Research has shown that listening to this music can accelerate learning.[219]
- Temporarily block social media and updates on your phone using third party apps such as *Freedom*. Uninterrupted focus is essential to achieving the flow state. Constant digital updates make flow state impossible.
- Attach risk to what you are doing, whether it be financial risk or risk to your reputation. Science shows that risk increases the likelihood we will enter the flow state.[220]

As you read this, your inner voice might be expressing skepticism about this actually working. It's understandable that it wouldn't be on board. You are about to press the button to activate the ejector seat and send it flying out of your brain into thin air.

You're trying to evict the inner voice from your mind.

No wonder it's worried.

ERIC AND BRET WEINSTEIN

25. LABORATORY RATS HAVE SHORTENED HUMAN LIFE

TOPIC: SCIENCE
GUEST: SCIENTIST & MATHEMATICIAN
PODCAST: #1006, #1203, #1320, #1494+
WHERE TO FIND MORE: THE PORTAL (PODCAST), DARKHORSE (PODCAST)

The next idea is embedded in a story about mutant mice, deceit, a Nobel Prize and bias in drug research that might be responsible for prematurely ending human life. It is the first time this story has ever been formally investigated for the general public. The fact that a self-publishing undergraduate author is the person to do so speaks to the heart of what it is all about. The idea is called the *Distributed Idea Suppression Complex* (DISC) by Harvard mathematician and hedge fund manager Eric Weinstein. Both Eric and his brother Bret Weinstein have featured on the podcast but Eric's podcast, *The Portal* is essential viewing and where this story was first told.[221]

Despite the complex name that sounds awfully like a conspiracy theory, the idea is actually fairly simple. It is that mainstream institutions have censored ideas that do not fit with their institutional narratives. On the surface, this seems obvious as there is already immense distrust of mainstream media and government, especially from Joe Rogan listeners. Weinstein however, more provocatively claims this suppression of ideas is occurring within the scientific community itself – the institution responsible for arguably the greatest human achievement of all time, the scientific method. Science's unapologetic search for truth has revealed more about the cosmos than any prophet, oracle or guru. The field has reduced human suffering through discoveries of modern medicine such as penicillin, the X-ray and vaccines. Science has defied the fate of our species and given each of us more revolutions around the Sun. Now this same institution has become endangered as human ego causes the system to pose a danger to the very humans it sought to help. The scientific establishment faces a crisis as new ideas are suppressed by toxic old practices.

To help us unpack this idea, let me tell you a story. The year is 1999. A time of Nokias, Harry Potter books, the Backstreet Boys, *American Pie*, Britney Spears, terrible outfits and *The Matrix*. Amidst all this was a promising young graduate student studying biology at the University of Michigan. He sat in a lecture hall as another graduate student gave a presentation about cancer. While most of the students sat disinterestedly copying the material onto notepads, the young man suddenly froze. In that exact moment he had made a discovery that no one else in the world might have known. The ramifications of this discovery were so far-reaching that they undermined an entire field of science. The discovery meant that for decades humans had been consuming pharmaceutical drugs which were more toxic than believed. All because of a simple methodological flaw that might have been solved with one phone call. That graduate student's name was Bret Weinstein.

Today, Bret Weinstein is one of the few biologists of the 21st century with more than 100,000 followers on Twitter. The man even debated evolutionary biology with the greatest living biologist of our time, Richard Dawkins. It would seem safe to assume that back in 1999 Bret Weinstein's discovery would have made him a household name in the scientific community. You would be wrong. It did not. And this is where our story begins.

Bret Weinstein became a professor at an obscure liberal arts university called Evergreen State College. He was an unknown academic for almost his entire career – until 2017. How could a man who made a discovery worth a Nobel Prize be an unknown academic at some third-tier university and only rise to fame in 2017? The answer is completely unrelated to science. Since the 1970s, Evergreen State College had an annual tradition called the 'Day of Absence' where minority students would leave campus to highlight their contribution to the college. In 2017, the college asked all white students and faculty members to leave campus on the 'Day of Absence' in a strange act of reverse discrimination. Bret, a progressive Jewish male, refused to do so. Hordes of enraged students protested outside his lecture hall chanting for him to be fired. Videos of Bret trying to reason with the protestors and calmly express his argument went viral. He quickly became a poster child for the right to free speech in America. Bret Weinstein was famous. The world had discovered Bret yet Bret's discovery was still nowhere to be seen.

Let's go back to 1999. At the time, scientists were exploring something called telomeres and their role in cancer. Telomeres are like our genetic hourglass.[222] They are found at both ends of the 46 chromosomes that exist in all of the body's cells – like protective buffers on each end of our DNA sequence. Every time our cells divide – a process necessary to keep living – these protective buffers get worn down. However, an enzyme called telomerase, keeps trying to rebuild the buffer. But no matter how hard it tries, the rate of division is faster than the buffer can rebuild. The buffers or telomeres slowly but surely get shorter as we grow older. Eventually the telomeres become so short that they signal the cell to stop dividing. The cell has reached its Hayflick limit, the maximum number of cell divisions before it can no longer replicate. This is the process of aging or senescence as scientists call it. It's why old people have grey hair and wrinkled skin. Their cells can't replace themselves anymore.

In the lecture hall, Bret listened as the student talked about the role of cancer and telomeres. It turns out cancer knew about these telomeres too. Cancer's goal is to grow indefinitely and it needs cells to keep dividing to do that. It needs telomerase to keep the telomeres long. This would allow the chromosomes to be protected so no signal is made to stop dividing. Cancer wants your body's cells to be immortal. This was Bret's Eureka moment. What if cancer was the cost of immortality and death was the only protection against death? Our telomeres are in a tug of war between being so long that we are at risk of tumor formation, and being so short that we die of age-related causes. Evolution has carefully selected the trade-off that allows these forces to be in balance for the longest amount of time, letting us live as long as we can under this Sun.

It gets even more interesting.

Bret Weinstein's realization provided support for the theory of antagonistic pleiotropy in humans. Such a theory seems like you have to wear a monocle to understand it, yet, it is actually elegantly simple. Humans are incredibly complex organisms with trillions of cells and only a much smaller number of genes. In order for this complexity to exist, genes usually have to do more than one thing. This is called pleiotropy. A gene can have both positive and negative effects – if a gene has a positive effect in the early life of a human but has a negative effect later in life, the evolutionary process biases this gene. This is antagonistic pleiotropy.

A very simplified way to think about it is like smoking. You might smoke when you are young to look cool and attract a partner (this is an analogy not an accusation). But then when you're old and married with the girl who thought you were cool, you get lung cancer from the smoking you did when you were young. Why would evolution care? You have had a child, your job on Earth is done. Evolution biases this trade-off of genes that act favorably when you are young but harmfully when you are older because most people do not experience the harmful effects (they are already dead).

Telomeres provide evidence of this evolutionary concept of antagonistic pleiotropy in humans. This is because while longer telomere lengths are favorable in early life they increase our chance of tumor formation later in life.

Weinstein made a prediction. He predicted that, in environments where animals die mainly from external causes, evolution would be biased towards shorter telomere lengths because most animals will not live long enough to die from aging. This is what good science looks like – a prediction that you can prove right or wrong.

There was a big problem. Every scientist at the time knew mice lived short lives and had long telomeres. In fact, mice had far longer telomeres than humans yet lived for only a few years. Weinstein's theory had reached a roadblock. If his theory was correct, evolution would not have given mice long telomeres as they do not live long enough to need long telomeres to protect them from age-related diseases. It didn't make sense.

Then he had another crazy idea. Maybe it wasn't all mice that had long telomeres but it was just laboratory mice. He did some more research. Amazingly, almost every laboratory mouse in the United States came from one facility, the Jackson Laboratory (JAX) in Maine. Mice from the same place were being used to test drugs in the most prestigious universities around the country from John Hopkins University to Harvard Medical School.

As JAX proudly boast on their website, there are 30,000 peer-reviewed research articles where their rodents have been used. Weinstein called the laboratory and asked about how their breeding protocol worked to correct against evolutionary biases. The second Eureka moment. They didn't have one. JAX had to breed many mice as cheaply as possible. The beauty of the free market, Eric Weinstein jokes sarcastically on the podcast. Young mice breed faster than old mice. JAX would kill old mice and keep the young ones so the breeding rate was as high as possible. No scientist in the entire country realized that every mouse in their own laboratories had been altered by evolution and the free market. The selection process at JAX biased genes that expressed favorably when they were young and harmful when they were old. Because the mice didn't reach old age it didn't matter if they had some genes which would be a ticking time bomb later.

Weinstein realized the breeding protocol of this single laboratory had, over the course of many mice generations, made their telomeres longer. This meant that the rodents used for almost all initial drug trials had been turned into mutants that did not serve as accurate models for humans. This breeding protocol meant the mice could absorb immense damage because of their superhuman telomeres. So the studies provided data that drastically understated how toxic these drugs would be to humans.

A skeptic might say that mouse models are never going to be accurate for humans. We are different. The reality is that these are the best animals to use as their short life spans allow us to test the long term effects of a drug in a short period of time. Think of how few medications would be available if researchers had to wait decades for the results to come through. And with a single change in breeding protocol, thousands of clinical trials could be more accurate and undoubtedly help protect humans from the understated toxic effects of pharmaceutical drugs. It could have been solved with a phone call.

Bret knew he was onto something. And this is where the story gets ugly. The young graduate student was in way over his head and he needed someone who knew something about telomeres. There was no better person than Carol Greider. She was a household name in the field for her discovery of telomerase in 1984 and she would go on to win the Nobel Prize for Medicine in 2009. Bret called Carol.

"Do you think it's possible that laboratory mice have far longer telomeres than mice in the wild?"

That decision would be one of the biggest mistakes of his career. Although we cannot know for certain what Carol said on that phone call over twenty years ago, we do know she was indeed interested in Weinstein's hypothesis. So interested in fact that her laboratory at John Hopkins University did the experiment.[223] The results came back. Incredibly the telomeres of wild mice were shorter. Weinstein was right. He had predicted through first principles observable results in molecular biology. It was a breakthrough. Greider called Weinstein with the news.

Frantically he got to work on his paper so it could be shared with the world. His paper made a series of predictions and Carol Greider's lab had just confirmed one of them. She was part of the scientific establishment and her approval would catapult him into mainstream success.

Eventually the paper was finished. Weinstein sent the paper to Carol Greider for feedback. She slammed it. Her criticism extended to virtually every sentence on the page. Weinstein was in disbelief at what he described as, "not sensible feedback." This was strange as Weinstein had assumed that Greider was an ally, she had after all confirmed his prediction. He became suspicious.

He completed his paper for publication. For the paper to be published it needed to be submitted to a scientific journal and go through the process of peer review. This is the process in science where peers in the field review your work to see if it is worthy of going to publication. The paper was submitted to *Nature*. They declined it.[224] They said they did not think their readers would be interested in a paper showing mutant mice were interfering with most drug trials in America. Weinstein was a no one – he needed Carol Greider.

He called Carol again and asked if she would release the finding that laboratory mice had longer telomeres than wild mice. She said the paper was completed and he asked to see it. She sent him a manuscript without graphs or acknowledgments – this was strange. He asked her to send the acknowledgments and his name was nowhere to be seen. Weinstein asked why he was not acknowledged as a co-author. "I have no history of an email with you sending any hypothesis," Carol replied.

He had called her not emailed her. There was no written record of his prediction. When I read his paper that was finally published in 2002, buried in there is the following: "One of us predicted to Greider that long telomeres in laboratory mice would be atypical for mice in general."[225] That was written about twenty years ago and Bret's story has not changed. It seems unlikely a young scientist would include it if it was false as it would jeopardize his entire career and make him subject to claims of academic misconduct.

It seems Greider did not want this paper to get attention. His theory, which was one of the only evolutionary theories of the last hundred years to make a prediction from first principles which had been observed at the molecular level, had just lost all its firepower. Without Greider's support, Weinstein remained an unknown graduate student whose theories questioned the scientific validity of 30,000 plus studies. His paper was published by an obscure scientific journal where it went largely unnoticed.[226] It's hardly a surprise this happened. The sheer number of careers, let alone egos, that the finding threatened meant the establishment would not take notice.

You can find Bret's paper on the internet under the title *The Reserve Capacity Hypothesis.*[227] You can also find Carol Greider's 2009 Nobel Prize lecture on YouTube.[228] That same paper that she slammed, the one she refused to allow into the mainstream, seems to align with all of her recent research.[229] This might look like libel but anyone with an internet connection can look at the same two sources I have cited and the dates of Greider's later work. She seems to agree with everything that Weinstein predicted all those years ago. If she really did slam Weinstein's paper initially, the continued lack of acknowledgment looks like academic misconduct at a serious level. The only prediction she seems not to agree with is the damage that drugs were causing on humans because of using flawed mouse models that could be easily fixed. It seems this is the one prediction she was not brave enough to borrow. The field of science could not acknowledge that for the years testing was done on these rodents, their elongated telomeres enabled them to absorb levels of toxicity that humans simply could not. The one prediction which challenged the entire scientific establishment.

Lo and behold – the evidence supports Bret Weinstein. Vioxx, a drug released to treat arthritis, was tested on mice as all of these drugs are. The drug is estimated to have caused over 130,000 heart attacks in its users, with 60,000 dying.[230] There are countless other drugs that have been recalled. It is not a coincidence that these drugs are causing damage to organs known to have little cell repair. Telomeres. The effects these drugs have are not picked up in rodent studies because humans cannot repair themselves at the level of these mutant mice.

This story is about the *Distributed Idea Suppression Complex.* The scientific institution is not the transparent golden child we thought it was. Human ego is entwined with the institution in a toxic way. Bold new ideas are trapped as the fiercely competitive scientific landscape sees those in a position of power halt those who threaten them. Bret was a nobody; Carol was a somebody.

The process of peer review is not just criticized by the Weinstein brothers. An article released by a long-time editor of a prominent science publication blasted the very process he was a part of.[231] He acknowledges that it is not uncommon for peer reviewers to give unjust reviews so that their competition does not publish their ideas. It makes sense. Why would someone want their peers' paper to be published if it contradicted their work? Especially if it meant they might not get the grant they need to keep their livelihood.

In a world where the stakes of inaction affect the fate of our species, we need an effective system that allows the best ideas to rise to the top. The marriage of human ego and bureaucracy is the number one enemy of ingenuity. It's why you might be consuming a drug that is aging you without you even knowing it. It is the reason you just heard of Bret Weinstein.

ACKNOWLEDGMENTS

Humans really are just apes. And no single ape could write a book without the help of those other apes around them.

First and foremost, thank you to Joe Rogan and Jamie Vernon for providing a free education to the masses. Without their platform a wealth of information and ideas would be hidden behind paywalls and expensive college degrees.

Thank you to my editor Harriet Richert for her incredible ability to improve my writing, calling me out on bullshit and believing in the project from the start. Thank you to the incredible design team at Studio 3:AM, led by Jonathan Key and Cathy Nguyen who created all the graphic designs for the book including the incredible cover design. A huge thanks to Frances O'Brien for her work on marketing the book, she has been amazing. I could not have made the book without these people.

And now the biggest thank you of all, my parents, Mandy and Andy. Your unwavering support, dedication, passion, care and love has been unmatched. For over fifty-year-olds to read about psychedelics, sex and hunting and always go into it with open minds has been inspiring. I love you two more than the universe. To my nan, thank you for believing in me. Thank you to Kelly, my sister, for always being supportive.

To William Cesta, thank you for planting the seed in my mind that I could do something different. Thank you to my teachers over the years Karen Yager, Vanessa Bromhead, Michael Griffiths, Maria Jobson and John Larkin. You have all been inspiring in different ways.

Finally, thank you to my friends. This book has been written on friends' couches from Byron Bay all the way to Lightning Ridge in Australia. Special thanks to the Gotterson and Cheal families for having me. Thanks to Max

Cutrone for coming up with the name of the book and Rory Cheal for coming up with the subtitle. A huge thanks to Nick Stillone for helping me record the Audible version of this book. Thanks to all the people who read draft chapters and provided feedback, Jasper Gotterson, Matt Stafford, Flynn Stallworthy, Jesse Hughes, Tom Humphrey, Jack Grant, Jamie Hepburn, Kevin Honan, Muiris Rowsome and Dern Garing. To all the other people after I have written this who have helped out, thank you. Mainly looking at the Knox boys and St Andrew's community. I know you shouldn't say anything bad in the acknowledgments but Honi Soit you can respectfully get fucked.

Finally, thank you to the JRE fans for always being curious and being part of a revolution that changed media. I hope you enjoyed the book.

NOTES

CHAPTER 1 - DR CARL HART

[1] **An article that contains the link to the allegations that George W. Bush did cocaine at Camp David. This is not confirmed but the allegations were put forward by a biographer of the family. See,** O'Cleary , C. (2013, February 24). An acute sense of rumor. Retrieved from https://www.irishtimes.com/news/an-acute-sense-of-rumor-1.1160186

[2] **General history of the drug war. See,** Drug Policy Alliance. (n.d.). A Brief History of the Drug War. Retrieved March 25, 2020, from https://www.drugpolicy.org/issues/brief-history-drug-war

[3] **Original quote from Nixon's top aide. See,** Baum, D. (2016, April 1). Legalize it All: How to win the war on drugs. *Harper's Magazine.* Retrieved from https://harpers.org

[4] **Quote about different doses of crack cocaine. See,** Hart, C. (2014). *High Price: A Neuroscientist's Journey of Self-Discovery That Challenges Everything You Know About Drugs and Society (P.S.)* (Reprint ed.). New York , United States: Harper Perennial, p192.

[5] **Source confirming similarity of crack and powdered cocaine. See,** Oxford Treatment Center. (2019, August 27). Difference Between Crack and Cocaine. Retrieved March 26, 2020, from https://www.oxfordtreatment.com/substance-abuse/cocaine/crack-vs-cocaine/

[6] **Independent discussion of medical literature. See,** Oxford Treatment Center. (2019, August 27). Difference Between Crack and Cocaine. Retrieved March 26, 2020, from https://www.oxfordtreatment.com/substance-abuse/cocaine/crack-vs-cocaine/

[7] **91 percent of people imprisoned due to anti-crack laws in 1991 were black. See,** US Sentencing Commission, Report to the Congress: Cocaine and Federal Sentencing Policy, May 2007, p16.

[8] **Excellent analysis of inability of drug war to reduce supply of drugs. See,** Coyne, C. J., & Hall, A. R. (2017, April 12). *Four decades and counting: The continued failure of the war on drugs.* Retrieved from https://www.cato.org/publications/policy-analysis/four-decades-counting-continued-failure-war-drugs

[9] **The definition of addiction is that drug use must take over someone's life. See,** American Psychiatric Association. *Diagnostic and Statistical Manual of Mental Disorders - DSM 5.* Washington DC:American Psychiatric Association; 2013.

[10] **Note I could not find the academic source for this statistic but managed to find the article that confirmed statistics. See,** Hart, C. *High Price,* p211; Tierney, J. (2013, September 16). The Rational Choices of Crack Addicts. *The New York Times.* Retrieved from https://www.nytimes.com

[11] **Percent of alcohol users who will gain an addiction. See,** American Addiction Centers Resource. (2020, April 15). Alcoholism statistics & Alcohol Abuse Demographics. Retrieved May 20, 2020, from https://www.alcohol.org/statistics-information/

[12] **Dr Carl Hart outlines his personal research into methamphetamine. See,** Hart, p. *High Price,* p302-304; Hart CL, Marvin CB, Silver R, Smith EE. *Is cognitive functioning impaired in methamphetamine users?* A critical review. Neuropsychopharmacology. 2012;37:586.

[13] **Graph on the harm different drugs cause to society. See,** *The Economist.* (2019, June 28). What is the most dangerous drug? Retrieved from https://www.economist.com

[14] **Discussion of Portugal's drug laws. See**, Hart, C. *High Price,* p324-326.

CHAPTER 2 - NEIL DEGRASSE TYSON

[15] **JFK's famous speech. See,** NASA. (1962, September 12). *JFK RICE MOON SPEECH* [Press release]. Retrieved June 17, 2020, from https://er.jsc.nasa.gov/seh/ricetalk.htm#:%7E:text=We%20choose%20to%20go%20to%20the%20moon%20in%20this%20decade,to%20postpone%2C%20and%20one%20which

[16] **Nixon's speech if the moon landing was a failure. See,** Economy, P. (2020, February 6). If Apollo 11 Had Crashed, Here's the Stunning Speech President Nixon Would Have Given the Nation (It's Always Good to Have a Plan B). Retrieved from https://www.inc.com/peter-economy/if-apollo-11-had-crashed-heres-stunning-speech-president-nixon-would-have-given-nation-its-always-good-to-have-a-plan-b.html

[17] **The first sentence from NDT's book. See,** deGrasse Tyson, N. (2017). *Astrophysics for People in a Hurry* (Revised ed.). New York, United States: W. W. Norton & Company, p1.

[18] **Excellent video concisely explaining the big bang. See,** *New Scientist.* (2017, March 23). *Lawrence Krauss explains the universe in less than 2 minutes*[Video file]. Retrieved from https://www.youtube.com/watch?v=QsLCs8vR2VE

[19] **Not available to the public but private university notes that informed my understanding. Request if possible from,** van de Sande, J. (2018, January 1). Lecture 31 - Galaxy Evolution [Slides]. Retrieved from https://www.sydney.edu.au/science/our-research/research-centres/sydney-institute-for-astronomy.html

[20] **Direct quotes about the guts of stars. See,** Tyson, *Astrophysics for People in a Hurry*, p29.

[21] **Stardust quote from Krauss. See,** Krauss, L. M., & Dawkins, R. (2013). *A Universe from Nothing: Why There Is Something Rather than Nothing* (unknown ed.). London , United Kingdom: Simon & Schuster, p17.

[22] **Grains of sand and stars in the universe. See,** Tyson, *Astrophysics for People in a Hurry*, p202.

[23] **Discussion of Earth's chemically rich oceans. See,** Tyson, *Astrophysics for People in a Hurry*, p30.

[24] **Jupiter as Earth's protective shield. See,** Tyson, *Astrophysics for People in a Hurry*, p176.

[25] **In a trillion years, other galaxies will be undetectable. See,** Tyson, *Astrophysics for People in a Hurry*, p112.

[26] **Discussion of the cosmic perspective. See,** Tyson, *Astrophysics for People in a Hurry*, p202.

[27] **Direct quote. See,** Tyson, *Astrophysics for People in a Hurry*, p203.

CHAPTER 3 - EDWARD SNOWDEN

[28] **The quote comes from Snowden's book. Interesting discussion of the old school CIA operatives. See,** Snowden, E. (2019). *Permanent Record.* London, United Kingdom: Metropolitan Books, p150.

[29] **Story of CIA agent reporting the Saudi financier. See,** Snowden, *Permanent Record*, p159.

[30] **Essay on the 'deep state' written by authors who were involved in this bureaucracy. Not great reading but the authors admit that agencies**

pursue their objectives over government interests. See, Cooper, D. A., Gvosdev, N. K., & Blankshain, J. D. (2018). Deconstructing the "Deep State": Subordinate Bureaucratic Politics in U.S. National Security. *Orbis*, *62*(4), 518–540. https://doi.org/10.1016/j.orbis.2018.08.009

[31] **The XKEYSCORE program is discussed. See,** Snowden, *Permanent Record*, p278.

[32] **The anecdote of Snowden hearing the child's laughter. See,** Snowden, *Permanent Record*, p282.

[33] **The constitution exists to make law enforcement jobs harder. See,** Snowden, *Permanent Record*, p228.

[34] **Discussion of China's social credit system. See,** Zhou , C. (2020, January 2). "We are basically living naked": The complicated truth about China's Social Credit System. Retrieved from https://www.abc.net.au/news/2020-01-02/china-social-credit-system-operational-by-2020/11764740

CHAPTER 4 - MATTHEW WALKER

[35] **Discussion of Edison's sleeping habits, should be noted that while his naps are well documented, metal ball bearings seem to be anecdotal. See,** Khazan, O. (2014, May 14). *Thomas Edison and the Cult of Sleep Deprivation.* Retrieved February 20, 2020, from https://www.theatlantic.com/health/archive/2014/05/thomas-edison-and-the-cult-of-sleep-deprivation/370824/

[36] **For statistic of six years of sleep, basic calculation can be made based off fact humans have two hours of dreams per night. See,** National Institute of Neurological Disorders and Stroke. (n.d.). *Brain Basics: Understanding Sleep.* Retrieved March 24, 2020, from https://www.ninds.nih.gov/Disorders/Patient-Caregiver-Education/Understanding-Sleep

[37] **Regions activated during sleep. See,** Walker, W. (2018). *Why We Sleep: Unlocking the Power of Sleep and Dreams* (Reprint ed.). New York , United States: Scribner, p223.

[38] **Dreams as emotional therapy. See**, Walker, *Why We Sleep*, p238.

[39] **Discussion about noradrenaline. See,** Walker, *Why We Sleep*, p239.

[40] **Experiment conducted by Walker's laboratory. See,** Walker, *Why We Sleep*, p241; Yoo, S. S., Gujar, N., Hu, P., Jolesz, F. A., & Walker, M. P. (2007a). *The human emotional brain without sleep – a prefrontal amygdala disconnect.* Curr. Biol., 17, R877–R878.

[41] **Studies that show sleep enhances creativity. See,** Walker, *Why We Sleep*, p250.

[42] **Reduced sleep leading to reduced testosterone. See,** Leproult R, Van CE. *Effect of 1 week of sleep restriction on testosterone levels in young healthy men.* JAMA. 2011;305:2173–4.

[43] **Statistic about people not meeting eight hours sleep requirement. See,** Walker, *Why We Sleep*, p1.

[44] **Daylight savings and heart attack evidence were first heard here. See,** TED. (2019, June 4). Sleep is Your Superpower Matthew Walker [Videofile]. *YouTube.*Retrieved from https://www.youtube.com/watch?v=5MuIMqhT8DM

[45] **General scientific discussion on the consequences of poor sleep. See,** Walker, *Why We Sleep*, p186-195.

[46] **Sleep's impact on athletic performance. See,** Takeuchi, g. m. Davis, M. Plyley, R. Goode & Roy J. Shephard (1985) *Sleep deprivation, chronic exercise and muscular performance*, Ergonomics, 28:3, 591-601.

[47] **Sleep's impact on memory. See,** Walker M.P. *The role of slow wave sleep in memory processing.* J. Clin. Sleep. Med. 2009;5(Suppl. 2): S20–S26.

[48] **Full list of sleep strategies. See,** Walker, *Why We Sleep*, Appendix.

CHAPTER 5 - CHRISTOPHER RYAN

[49] **Study that shows males accept sex far more than females. See,** Ryan, C., & Jetha, C. (2011) Sex at Dawn (Reprint ed.). New York, United States: Harper Perennial. p52; Clark and Hatfield (1989).

[50] **Controversial argument about hotness and beauty. See,** Rogan J, (JRE Clips). (2018, February 21*) Joe Rogan – The Science of Hotness vs. Beauty.* Retrieved by https://www.youtube.com/watch?v=PvQrFBOyDs0&t=111s

[51] **Genital swelling of primates reference first read in Ryan's work. See,** Ryan, *Sex at Dawn*, p59.

[52] **Discussion of standard sexual narrative. See,** Helen Fisher, *The Sex Contract: The Evolution of Human Behavior* (New York: William Morrow, 1982).

[53] **1.6 percent of DNA shared with chimpanzee. See,** Ryan, *Sex at Dawn*, p69.

[54] **Frequency that bonobos have sex. See,** Ryan, *Sex at Dawn*, p62.

[55] **Anthropological evidence against standard narrative of sexuality. See,** Ryan, *Sex at Dawn*, p91; Beckerman and Valentine (2002), p6.

[56] **Sperm competition idea heavily criticized. See,** Saxon, L. (2012). *Sex at Dusk*. Lexington, Kentucky: Createspace Independent Pub, p364.

CHAPTER 6 - DAVID GOGGINS

[57] **Great source material to learn about stoicism. See,** E. (1994). *A Manual for Living (Little Book of Wisdom (Harper San Francisco))* (1st ed.). New York , US: HarperOne, p11.

[58] **Original quote. See,** Goggins, D. (2018). *Can't Hurt Me: Master your mind and Defy Odds*. New York, United States: Lioncrest.

CHAPTER 7 - PAUL STAMETS

[59] **More microbial life in a hand of dirt than North America vertebrates and plants. See,** Stamets, P. (2005). *Mycelium Running: How Mushrooms Can Help Save the World* (1st Edition). New York , United States: Ten Speed Press, p1.

[60] **Statistic about loss of bio-diversity. See,** Paul Stamets, *Mycelium Running*, p116.

[61] **Original claim made by Stamets on podcast. Widely supported as evidenced by the following internet article. See,** King, A. (2019, February 18). NPR Choice page. Retrieved from https://choice.npr.org/index.html?origin=https://www.npr.org/sections/thesalt/2019/02/18/694301239/massive-loss-of-thousands-of-hives-afflicts-orchard-growers-and-beekeepers

[62] **Article that cites the expert belief that about 35 percent of crops directly depend upon bee pollination. See,** Fairfax. (2018, November 16). Fact check: Is two-thirds of Australia's food production reliant on bee pollination? Retrieved from https://www.abc.net.au/news/2018-10-15/fact-check-honey-bee-pollination/10365750?nw=0

[63] **300 miles of Mycelium underneath each footstep. See**, Paul Stamets, *Mycelium Running*, p10.

[64] **Japanese slime mold experiment. See,** American Association for the Advancement of Science. (2010, January 22). Slime design mimics Tokyo's rail system: Efficient methods of a slime mold could inform human engineers. *ScienceDaily*. Retrieved June 2, 2020 from www.sciencedaily.com/releases/2010/01/100121141051.htm

[65] **First mushrooms to grow. See,** Paul Stamets, *Mycelium Running*, p55.

[66] **Mycelium steering the selection of species in the ecosystem. See,** Paul Stamets, *Mycelium Running*, p4.

[67] **Stamets article in *Nature*. See,** Stamets, P.E., Naeger, N.L., Evans, J.D. et al. *Extracts of Polypore Mushroom Mycelia Reduce Viruses in Honey Bees*. Sci Rep 8, 13936 (2018). https://doi.org/10.1038/s41598-018-32194-8

[68] **Stamet's septic tank and use of mycelium as a filtration system. See,** Paul Stamets, *Mycelium Running*, p60.

CHAPTER 8 - JORDAN PETERSON

[69] **YouTube video of pronouns. See,** Katrina Fleming. (2016, October 12) *Jordan Peterson Swarmed by Narcissistic SJW Ideologues after UofT Rally*. Retrieved from https://www.youtube.com/watch?v=O-nvNAcvUPE

[70] **Explanation of the Grievance Studies. This involved submitting Mein Kampf (Hitler's book) and replacing Jew with male. It was accepted by academic journals in humanities departments. It highlights postmodernisms' willingness to reverse discriminate against anyone who is a male.** Pluckrose, H. (2019, March 18). Retrieved from https://www.theaustralian.com.au/r mote/check_cookie.html?url=https%3a%2f%2fwww.theaustralian.com.au%2fcommentary%2fthe-problem-with-grievance-studies%2fnews-story%2f674aefae465c3b26b9690f2997510d33

[71] **Heavily relied on this source for all original scientific content on lobsters. See,** Jordan Peterson, *12 Rules for Life: An Antidote to Chaos* (Canada: Random House, 2018), p1-12

[72] **Specific references to octopamine. See,** Peterson, *12 Rules for Life, p6.*

[73] **Lobsters respond to Prozac. See,** Huber, R., Smith, K., Delago, A., Isaksson, K., & Kravitz, E. A. (1997). Serotonin and aggressive motivation in crustaceans: altering the decision to retreat. *Proceedings of the National Academy of Sciences of the United States of America, 94*(11), 5939–5942. https://doi.org/10.1073/pnas.94.11.5939

[74] **Definitive evidence for stress harming immune system. See,** Segerstrom, S. C. & Miller, G. E. Psychological stress and the human immune system: a meta-analytic study of 30 years of inquiry. *Psychol. Bull.* 130, 1–37 (2004).

CHAPTER 9 - MICHAEL POLLAN

[75] **The source which states there is no evidence for Lewis Carroll's drugs use. See,** Is Alice in Wonderland really about drugs? (2012, August 20). *BBC News*. Retrieved from https://www.bbc.com

[76] **Mayans' use of psychedelics. See,** De Rios, M., Alger, N., Crumrine, N., Furst, P., Harman, R., Hellmuth, N., Wescott, R. (1974). The Influence of Psychotropic Flora and Fauna on Maya Religion [and Comments and Reply]. *Current Anthropology, 15*(2), 147-164. Retrieved May 17, 2020, from www.jstor.org/stable/2740991

[77] **The use of peyote cactus by Native Americans. See,** Horgan, J. (2017, July 5). Tripping on Peyote in Navajo Nation. Retrieved from https://blogs.scientificamerican.com/cross-check/tripping-on-peyote-in-navajo-nation/

[78] **Smoked venom toad produces DMT. See,** Pollan, M. (2019). *How to Change your Mind: The New Science of Psychedelics.* New York, United States: Penguin Random House, p272.

[79] **Psychedelics are non-addictive and have no known toxic dose. See,** Pollan, *How to Change your Mind*, p14.

[80] **Original article that introduced mushrooms to the West. See,** Wasson, R. Gordon. *Seeking the Magic Mushroom* Life magazine, May 13, 1957.

[81] **Study for smoking addiction and psilocybin. See,** Garcia-Romeu, A. P., Johnson, M. W., and Griffiths, R. R. (2014). Examining the psychological mechanisms of psilocybin-assisted smoking cessation treatment: a pilot study. *Drug Alcohol Depend.* 140:e66. doi: 10.1016/j.drugalcdep.2014.02.200

[82] **Evidence that LSD is effective in treating alcoholism. See**, Krebs, T. S., & Johansen, P.-Ø. (2012). Lysergic acid diethylamide (LSD) for alcoholism: meta-analysis of randomized controlled trials. *Journal of Psychopharmacology*, 26(7),994–1002.https://doi.org/10.1177/0269881112439253

[83] **NYU study of terminally ill patients and psilocybin. See,** Ross, S., Bossis, A., Guss, J., Agin-Liebes, G., Malone, T., Cohen, B., Schmidt, B. L. (2016). Rapid and sustained symptom reduction following psilocybin treatment for anxiety and depression in patients with life-threatening cancer: a randomized controlled trial. *Journal of Psychopharmacology*, 30(12), 1165–1180. https://doi.org/10.1177/0269881116675512

[84] **Excellent discussion of neuroscience literature. See,** Pollan, *How to Change your Mind*, p291-330.

[85] **Researchers likening the perspective of someone on psychedelics to being a child. See,** Pollan, *How to Change your Mind*, p328.

CHAPTER 10 - NICK BOSTROM

[86] **These are the options laid out in Bostrom's paper. The paper was the first fully formulated argument for humans living in a simulation. See,** Bostrom, N. (2003), "Are You Living in a Computer Simulation?" *Philosophical Quarterly* 53 (211), p1.

[87] **Exponential growth statistic. Bostrom's book is highly technical and would not recommend for recreational reading. See,** Bostrom, N. (2016). *Superintelligence: Paths, Dangers, Strategies* (Reprint ed.). London, United Kingdom: Oxford University Press, p2.

[88] **Discussion of Moore's Law. See,** Nick Bostrom, *Superintelligence*, p32.

[89] **Timeline of the improvements in the computer. See,** Computer History Museum. (2015, January 1). Computers | Timeline of Computer History | Computer History Museum. Retrieved from https://www.computerhistory.org/timeline/computers/

[90] **Contains a table of all games where AI has exceeded human ability. See,** Nick Bostrom, *Superintelligence*, p16.

[91] **When machine intelligence is expected to match human intelligence. See,** Nick Bostrom, *Superintelligence*, p23.

[92] **Great analytical work where Bostrom demonstrates how much faster future AI would be than humans. See,** Nick Bostrom, *Superintelligence*, p72.

[93] **Bostrom lays out what is required for brain emulation. See,** Nick Bostrom, *Superintelligence*, p36.

[94] **Assumption of Bostrom's argument. See,** Bostrom, N. (2003), "Are You Living in a Computer Simulation?" *Philosophical Quarterly* 53 (211), p2.

[95] **Direct quote. Sums up the position well. See,** Bostrom, N. (2003), "Are You Living in a Computer Simulation?" Philosophical Quarterly 53 (211), p14.

CHAPTER 11 - STEVEN PINKER

[96] **Excellent book which details the availability heuristic in greater depth. See,** Kahneman, D. (2013). *Thinking, Fast and Slow* (1st ed.). New York, United States: Farrar, Straus and Giroux.

[97] **Violent death graph. See,** Pinker, S. (2012). *The Better Angels of Our Nature: Why Violence Has Declined* (Reprint ed.). New York, United States: Penguin Books, p187.

[98] **Twenty human atrocities graph. See,** Pinker, *The Better Angels of Our*

Nature, p235.

[99] **Genghis Khan joke is made in another episode. See,** Rogan, J (PowerfulJRE). (2018, October 2) *The Joe Rogan Experience #1177.* Retrieved from https://www.youtube.com/watch?v=Z-XkTcgWKPE

[100] **Discussion of medieval torture. See,** Steven Pinker, *The Better Angels of Our Nature*, p176.

[101] **Percentage of the population that were peasants. See,** The British Library. (2015, April 30). Peasants and their role in rural life. Retrieved from https://www.bl.uk/the-middle-ages/articles/peasants-and-their-role-in-rural-life#:%7E:text=In%20the%20Middle%20Ages%2C%20the,could%20be%20described%20as%20peasants.

[102] Steven Pinker, *The Better Angels of Our Nature*, p295.

[103] **Discussion of debt in history. See**, Steven Pinker, *The Better Angels of Our Nature* (London: Penguin Books, 2011), p187.

[104] **Direct quote. See,** Steven Pinker, *The Better Angels of Our Nature*, p811.

CHAPTER 12 - GRAHAM HANCOCK

[105] **Excellent overview of the history of humans. Our last ancestors died about 13,000 years ago. See,** Harari, Y. N. (2018). *Sapiens: A Brief History of Humankind* (Reprint ed.). New York, United States: Harper Perennial, p19.

[106] **The lifestyle of nomadic tribes with almost no group possessions. See,** Harari, *Sapiens*, p27.

[107] **Humans spread to the Arab Peninsula about 70,000 years ago. See,** Harari, *Sapiens*, p15.

[108] **The claim that humans migrated to North America 14,000 years ago. This is called the 'Clovis First' model. See,** Harari, *Sapiens*, p14.

[109] **Hancock explains the land migration theory into North America. Not controversial. See,** Hancock, G. (2019). *America Before: The Key to Earth's Lost Civilization.* London, United Kingdom: Hodder & Stoughton, p53.

[110] **The accounts of Spanish explorers going through the Amazon rainforest. See,** Hancock, *America Before*, p138.

[111] **Armies in the Amazon. The journal that Hancock cites is widely available online. See,** Hancock, *America Before*, p140.

[112] **Evidence that ancient cities are being uncovered in the Amazon.**

See, Amazon Jungle Once Home to Millions More Than Previously Thought. (2018, March 27). *National Geographic.* Retrieved from https://www.nationalgeographic.com

[113] **The scientific paper that dated Monte Verde. See,** Dillehay, T. D., Ocampo, C., Saavedra, J., Sawakuchi, A. O., Vega, R. M., Pino, M., ... Dix, G. (2015). New Archaeological Evidence for an Early Human Presence at Monte Verde, Chile. *PLOS ONE, 10*(11), e0141923. https://doi.org/10.1371/journal.pone.0141923

[114] **Obtained independent information about Gobekli Tepe here. See,** Curry, A. (2008, November 1). Gobekli Tepe: The World's First Temple? *Smithsonian Magazine.* Retrieved from https://www.smithsonianmag.com

[115] **An example of Graham Hancock making a basic mistake in field he does not fully understand. See,** Andrew White. (2019, April 25). "Squaring the circle" in the Amazon: Graham Hancock got it wrong [Video file]. *YouTube.* Retrieved from https://www.youtube.com/watch?v=AHSJ_2DL3gI

CHAPTER 13 - SEAN CARROLL

[116] **Excellent overview of quantum mechanics. See,** Quantum Theory - Full Documentary HD. (2014, May 25). [Video file]. *YouTube.* Retrieved from https://www.youtube.com/watch?v=CBrsWPCp_rs&t=1809s

[117] **First time paintball analogy was used although it required significant expansion in written form. Original source. See,** If You Don't Understand Quantum Physics, Try This! (2019, February 25). [Video file]. *YouTube.* Retrieved from https://www.youtube.com/watch?v=Usu9xZfabPM

[118] **Explained in Carroll's book. See,** Sean Carroll, *Something Deeply Hidden: Quantum Worlds and the Emergence of Spacetime* (London: Oneworld Publications, 2019), p19.

[119] **Great summary. See,** Schrödinger's cat: A thought experiment in quantum mechanics - Chad Orzel. (2014, October 14). [Video file]. *YouTube.* Retrieved from https://www.youtube.com/watch?v=UjaAxUO6-Uw

CHAPTER 14 - SEBASTIAN JUNGER

[120] **First mention of Skinwalkers was in Junger's book although he did not make comparisons to Aurora school shooter or the Joker. See,** Junger, S. (2016). *Tribe: On Homecoming and Belonging* (1st ed.). New York, United States: Twelve, p113.

[121] **Discussion of the threat that the lone gunman poses to society. See,** Junger, *Tribe*, p114.

[122] **The phrase "apocalyptically violent" is Junger's phrase. See,** Junger, *Tribe*, p117.

[123] **PTSD in Israeli soldiers opposed to U.S. soldiers. See,** Junger, *Tribe*, p96.

[124] **Junger's referencing is problematic as he does not cite the source of his statistics. I first found the statistic in his book and it seems plausible based on the literature. Original source unknown. See,** Junger, *Tribe*, p17; Valiño, Á. (2017, April 14). How Humans Are Shaping Our Own Evolution. *National Geographic*. Retrieved from https://www.nationalgeographic.com

[125] **Excellent book that goes into extensive detail of people on the frontier joining the Native Indians. See,** Gwynne, S. C. (2010). *Empire of the Summer Moon: Quanah Parker and the Rise and Fall of the Comanches, the Most Powerful Indian Tribe in American History* (1st ed.). New York, United States: Scribner.

[126] **Direct quote. See,** Pinker, *The Better Angels of our Nature*, p428; Why men love war: Broyles, 1984.

[127] **Anecdotal reports of veterans missing war. See,** Meshad, S. (2019, November 15). The Paradox of Missing War. Retrieved from https://nvf.org/paradox-missing-war/

[128] **Mental health goes down in times of crisis. See,** Junger, *Tribe*, p46.

[129] **UK psychiatric admissions went down during the Blitz. See,** Junger, *Tribe*, p47.

CHAPTER 15 - JONATHAN HAIDT

[130] **Professor labeled as racist by some students for a politely worded email using the word 'mold'. See,** Bodenner, C. (2015, November 12). Now Claremont McKenna. Retrieved April 10, 2020, from https://www.theatlantic.com/notes/2015/11/now-claremont-mckenna/415758/?page=1&oldest=true

[131] **Academic paper that students protested. See,** Singal, J. (2017, May 2). This Is What a Modern-Day Witch Hunt Looks Like. Retrieved from https://nymag.com/intelligencer/2017/05/transracialism-article-controversy.html

[132] **Peanut allergy argument first found here in Haidt's book. See,** J Haidt, J., & Lukinaoff, G. (2018). *The Coddling of the American Mind: How Good Intentions and Bad Ideas are Setting Up a Generation for Failure*. New York, United States: Penguin Random House, p20.

[133] **The authors cite the scientific evidence. See,** Haidt & Lukinaoff, *The Coddling of the American Mind*, p21; Du Toit G, Roberts G, Sayre PH, Bahnson HT, Radulovic S, Santos AF, et al. Randomized trial of peanut consumption in infants at risk for peanut allergy. N Engl J Med. 2015;372:803–13.

[134] **Useful context surrounding the term iGen and Safetyism. See,** Haidt & Lukinaoff, *The Coddling of the American Mind*, p30.

[135] **Famous studies on parenting styles. See**, Horvat, E. M., Weininger, E. B., & Lareau, A. (2003). From Social Ties to Social Capital: Class Differences in the Relations Between Schools and Parent Networks. *American Educational Research Journal, 40*(2), 319–351.

[136] **Statistic on affluence of college students. See,** Haidt & Lukinaoff, *The Coddling of the American Mind*, p88.

[137] **Book that discusses the concept of being 'antifragile'. See,** Taleb, N. N. (2012). *Antifragile: Things That Gain From Disorder.* New York, United States: Penguin Random House, p3.

[138] **Microaggression paper. See,** Wing, Capodilupo, Torino, Bucceri, Holder, Nadal, Esquilin (2007). Racial Microaggressions in Everyday Life: Implications for Clinical Practice. American Psychologist, 62, 4, 271-286

[139] **The New York Times article arguing that words can be a form of violence. See,** Barrett, L. F. (2017, July 15). When Is Speech Violence? *Https://Www.Nytimes.Com/#publisher.* Retrieved from https://www.nytimes.com

[140] **Logical error critiqued by authors. See,** Haidt & Lukinaoff, *The Coddling of the American Mind*, 95.

[141] **Statistics about depression and anxiety for iGen. See,** Haidt & Lukinaoff, *The Coddling of the American Mind*, p145.

[142] **Discussion about PTSD and trigger warning. See,** Haidt & Lukinaoff, *The Coddling of the American Mind*, p29.

CHAPTER 16 - DR CORNEL WEST

[143] **The unexamined life is not worth living. See,** (1979). Plato's Apology of Socrates: An interpretation, with a new translation. Ithaca, N.Y: Cornell University Press.

[144] **Slavery as the economic engine for the South. See,** Timmons, G. (2019, December 18). How Slavery Became the Economic Engine of the South. Retrieved from https://www.history.com/news/slavery-profitable-southern-economy

[145] **Direct quote. See,** President (1861-1865: Lincoln). The Emancipation Proclamation. Bedford, Mass. Applewood Books, 1998.

[146] **Fundamental crisis in the black community. See,** West, C. (2017). *Race Matters, 25th Anniversary: With a New Introduction* (Anniversary ed.). New York , United States: Beacon Press, p63.

[147] **Statistic about agriculture and employment. See,** West, *Race Matters*, p53.

[148] **Statistic about drug possession against drug conviction. See,** West, *Race Matters*, preface.

[149] **Single motherhood as a predictor of poverty. See,** Thompson, D. (2014, January 23). None. Retrieved from https://www.theatlantic.com/business/archive/2014/01/economists-your-parents-are-more-important-than-ever/283301/

[150] **Initially quoted by Bernie Sanders as 1 in 3 but closer inspection has put that number at around 1 in 4. See,** Kessler, G. (2015, June 16). The stale statistic that one in three black males born today will end up in jail. Retrieved from https://www.washingtonpost.com/gdpr-consent/?next_url=https%3a%2f%2fwww.washingtonpost.com%2fnews%2ffact-checker%2fwp%2f2015%2f06%2f16%2fthe-stale-statistic-that-one-in-three-black-males-has-a-chance-of-ending-up-in-jail%2f

[151] West, *Race Matters*, p3.

CHAPTER 17 - SAM HARRIS

[152] **Podcast where Harris explains argument clearly, great resource for understanding. See,** PowerfulJRE. (2014, October 3). "Thoughts" with Sam Harris (from Joe Rogan Experience #543) [Video file]. *YouTube*. Retrieved from https://www.youtube.com/watch?v=hxKR6gtkSYs

[153] **Analogy was first written in *The Happiness Hypothesis* but for summary. See,** Haidt, J., & Lukinaoff, G. (2018). *The Coddling of the American mind: How Good Intentions and Bad Ideas are Setting Up a Generation for Failure.* New York, United States: Penguin Random House, p35.

[154] **The psychological literature how reasoning usually occurs after intuition. See,** Patterson R., Rothstein J., Barbey A. K. (2012). Reasoning, cognitive control, and moral intuition. *Front. Integr. Neurosci.* 6:114

[155] **Excellent summary of split brain experiments. See,** Wolman, D. (2012). The Split Brain: A tale of two halves. *Nature, 483*(7389). Retrieved from https://www.nature.com/news/the-split-brain-a-tale-of-two-halves-1.10213

[156] **Idea that we might all be Sperry patients comes from Sam's book. See,** Sam Harris, Waking up: A Guide to Spirituality Without Religion (United States: Simon & Schuster, 2014), p66.

[157] **Consciousness can be divided into two physical points. See,** Harris, *Waking Up*, p74.

[158] **Discussion of Derek Parfit's thought experiments. See,** Harris, *Waking Up*, p84.

[159] **Direct quotation. See**, Harris, *Waking Up*, p88.

[160] **Meditation can alter grey matter in your brain. See,** Luders, E. et al. The unique brain anatomy of meditation practitioners: alterations in cortical gyrification. *Front. Hum. Neurosci.* 6, 34 (2012).

[161] **Meditation increasing pain threshold. See,** Harris, *Waking Up*, p8; Zeidan, F., Martucci, K. T., Kraft, R. A., Gordon, N. S., McHaffie, J. G., and Coghill, R. C. (2011). Brain mechanisms supporting the modulation of pain by mindfulness meditation. *J. Neurosci.* 31, 5540–5548.

CHAPTER 18 - CAMERON HANES

[162] **Source for the statistics of people's attitudes towards hunting in North America. See,** Byrd, E., Lee, J. G., & Widmar, N. (2017). Perceptions of Hunting and Hunters by U.S. Respondents. *Animals: an open access journal from MDPI*, *7*(11), 83. https://doi.org/10.3390/ani7110083

[163] **Survey of people's motives for hunting. See,** Human Dimensions . (2017, March 31). HDgov | Human Dimensions. Retrieved from https://my.usgs.gov/hd/news/proportion-american-hunters-who-say-they-hunt-mostly-meat-continues-grow

[164] **Excellent article where a reporter goes into a slaughterhouse. One in a hundred cows are not stunned. See,** This Is What Humane Slaughter Looks Like. Is It Good Enough? (2018, October 2). Retrieved from https://modernfarmer.com/2013/04/this-is-what-humane-slaughter-looks-like-is-it-good-enough/

[165] **National Geographic article about hunters and conservation. See.** Bittel, J. (2014, October 14). 4 Places Where Hunters Are Working to Protect Game Animals. Retrieved from https://www.nationalgeographic.com/news/2014/10/141015-hunters-conservation-science-animals-hunting-environment/

[166] **National Geographic article about trophy hunting. See,** Paterniti, M. Trophy Hunting: Should We Kill Animals to Save Them? (2017, November 18).

Retrieved from https://www.nationalgeographic.com/magazine/2017/10/trophy-hunting-killing-saving-animals/

[167] **The claim that hunting an elephant provides the financial resources to protect 2,500 more is from this source. See,** Paterniti, M. Trophy Hunting: Should We Kill Animals to Save Them? (2017, November 18). Retrieved from https://www.nationalgeographic.com/magazine/2017/10/trophy-hunting-killing-saving-animals/

CHAPTER 19 - ROBERT SAPOLSKY

[168] **Original reference to Charles Whitman. See,** Sapolsky, R. M. (2018). *Behave: The Biology of Humans at Our Best and Worst* (Reprint ed.). New York , United States: Penguin Books, p36.

[169] **Temperature of cup impacts character judgment. See,** Sapolsky, *Behave;* Williams LE, Bargh JA (2008) *Experiencing physical warmth promotes interpersonal warmth.* Science 322:606–607

[170] **Discussion of trolley problem and neuroscience. See,** Sapolsky, *Behave, 391-393;* Greene, J. 2016. Solving the Trolley Problem. *In A Companion to Experimental Philosophy,* ed. J. Sytsma and W. Buckwalter, 175–189. Malden, MA: Wiley Blackwell.

[171] **Extract of study with judicial sentencing . See,** Sapolsky, *Behave,* p 387.

[172] **Discussion of Toxoplasmosis. See,** Rogan, J (PowerfulJRE). (2017, May 12) *Joe Rogan Experience #965*

[173] **Scientific literature on toxoplasmosis and impulsivity. See,** Vyas, A., Kim, S.-K., Giacomini, N., Boothroyd, J. C. & Sapolsky, R. M. Behavioural changes induced by Toxoplasma infection of rodents are highly specific to aversion of cat odors. Proc. Natl. Acad. Sci. USA; Stock AK, Dajkic D, Köhling HL, von Heinegg EH, Fiedler M, Beste C. *Humans with latent toxoplasmosis display altered reward modulation of cognitive control.* SciRep. 2017;7:10170.

[174] **Sapolsky's view on free will and criminal justice system. See,** Sapolsky, *Behave,* p467-494.

CHAPTER 20 - S.C. GWYNNE

[175] **A must read book. Discussion of the Comanches' ability to hunt. See,** Gwynne, S. C. (2010). *Empire of the Summer Moon: Quanah Parker and the Rise and*

Fall of the Comanches, the Most Powerful Indian Tribe in American History (1st ed.). New York , United States: Scribner, p198.

[176] **Discussion of Spanish and Comanches. See,** S.C. Gwynne, *Empire of the Summer Moon*, p53.

[177] **The frontier of Texas. See,** S.C. Gwynne, *Empire of the Summer Moon*, p14.

[178] **Direct quote. See,** S.C. Gwynne, *Empire of the Summer Moon*, p20.

[179] **Famous speech. See,** S.C. Gwynne, *Empire of the Summer Moon*, p27.

[180] **The price of buffalo. General discussion of mass extermination. See,** S.C. Gwynne, *Empire of the Summer Moon*, p260.

CHAPTER 21 - DR RHONDA PATRICK

[181] **Statistics on obesity in America. See,** Hurt, R. T., Kulisek, C., Buchanan, L. A., & McClave, S. A. (2010). The obesity epidemic: challenges, health initiatives, and implications for gastroenterologists. *Gastroenterology & hepatology*, *6*(12), 780–792.

[182] **Child obesity in America. See,** General, O. O. T. S. (2020, June 23). Background on Obesity - The Surgeon General's Vision for a Healthy and Fit Nation - NCBI Bookshelf. Retrieved from https://www.ncbi.nlm.nih.gov/books/NBK44656/

[183] **Excellent book that formed the basis for much of the chapter. Statistic about chronic disease found here. See,** Stephen, L. (2017). *Eating Ourselves Sick: How modern food is destroying our health.* New York, United States: Macmillan Publishers, p29.

[184] **Origins of food pyramids. See,** Louise Stephen, *Eating Ourselves Sick*, p54.

[185] **Statistic that 38% of panel does not have nutritional expertise. See,** Louise Stephen, *Eating Ourselves Sick*, p57.

[186] **Meta-analysis of low carb diets vs low-fat diets. See,** Sackner-Bernstein, J., Kanter, D., & Kaul, S. (2015). Dietary Intervention for Overweight and Obese Adults: Comparison of Low-Carbohydrate and Low-Fat Diets. A Meta-Analysis. *PloS one*, *10*(10), e0139817. https://doi.org/10.1371/journal.pone.0139817

[187] **USDA admitted the flawed cholesterol hypothesis. See,** Louise Stephen, *Eating Ourselves Sick*, p56.

[188] **Ethnographic evidence. See,** Louise Stephen, *Eating Ourselves Sick*, p25.

CHAPTER 22 - JOHANN HARI

[189] **Scientific literature on the ineffectiveness of antidepressants. See,** Kirsch, I. (2014). *Antidepressants and the Placebo Effect. Z. Psychol.* 222, 128–134.

[190] **Discussion of depression and the chemical imbalance myth. See,** Hari, J. (2019). *Lost Connections: Why You're Depressed and How to Find Hope* (Reprint ed.). London, United Kingdom: Bloomsbury Publishing, p34-39.

[191] **The research linking suicide and antidepressants. See,** Nischal, A. Tripathi, A. Nischal, J.K. Trivedi *Suicide and antidepressants: What current evidence indicates* Mens Sana Monographs, 10 (2012), p33-44

[192] **Direct quote. See,** Hari, *Lost Connections,* p313.

[193] **Full list of factors to increase happiness. See,** Hari, *Lost Connections,* contents page.

[194] **The Michigan prison study that is mentioned in the book. See,** Hari, *Lost Connections,* p159; Frumkin H: *Beyond toxicity: Human health and the natural environment.* Am J Prev Med. 2001, 20: 234-240.

[195] **Study of dietary intervention and depression. See,** Jacka, F. N., O'Neil, A., Opie, R., Itsiopoulos, C., Cotton, S., Mohebbi, M., et al. (2017). *A randomised controlled trial of dietary improvement for adults with major depression (the 'SMILES' trial).* BMC Med. 15-23.

[196] Hari, *Lost Connections,* p73-87.

CHAPTER 23 - DAVID SINCLAIR

[197] **Statistic that finding a cure for cancer would only add 2.1 years of life. See,** PhD, D. S. A., & LaPlante, M. D. (2019). *Lifespan: Why We Age—and Why We Don't Have To* (1st ed.). New York , United States: Atria Books, p77.

[198] **Statistic that smoking causes a fivefold increase in chance of cancer as well as aging effects on likelihood of cancer. See,** Sinclair, *Lifespan,* p80.

[199] **Statistic that over eighty-five-year olds can expect to be diagnosed with five diseases. See,** Sinclair, *Lifespan,* p79

[200] **Sinclair's own research that extended the life of mice with resveratrol. See,** Baur, J. A., Pearson, K. J., Price, N. L., Jamieson, H. A., Lerin, C., Kalra, A., Prabhu, V. V., Allard, J. S., Lopez-Lluch, G., Lewis, K., Pistell, P. J., Poosala, S., Becker, K. G., Boss, O., Gwinn, D., Wang, M., Ramaswamy, S., Fishbein, K. W., Spencer, R. G., Lakatta, E. G., … Sinclair, D. A. (2006). Resveratrol improves health and survival of mice on a high-caloric diet. *Nature, 444*(7117), 337–342. https://doi.

org/10.1038/nature05354

[201] **Eating less increases longevity. See,** Sinclair, *Lifespan*, p94.

[202] **Great overview of research into intermittent fasting in humans. See,** Patterson, R. E., Laughlin, G. A., LaCroix, A. Z., Hartman, S. J., Natarajan, L., Senger, C. M., Martínez, M. E., Villaseñor, A., Sears, D. D., Marinac, C. R., & Gallo, L. C. (2015). Intermittent Fasting and Human Metabolic Health. *Journal of the Academy of Nutrition and Dietetics, 115*(8), 1203–1212. https://doi.org/10.1016/j.jand.2015.02.018

[203] **Exercise and longevity. See,** Sinclair, *Lifespan*, p104.

[204] **A non-biased and comprehensive look into all research about the health benefits of Sauna. See,** Hussain, J., & Cohen, M. (2018). Clinical Effects of Regular Dry Sauna Bathing: A Systematic Review. *Evidence-based complementary and alternative medicine : eCAM, 2018*, 1857413. https://doi.org/10.1155/2018/1857413

[205] **Benefits of being cold. See,** Sinclair, *Lifespan*, p108.

[206] **Discussion of resveratrol see,** Sinclair, *Lifespan*, p304.

[207] **Metformin shown to reduce biological age. See,** Fahy, GM, Brooke, RT, Watson, JP, et al. Reversal of epigenetic aging and immunosenescent trends in humans. *Aging Cell.* 2019; 18:e13028. https://doi.org/10.1111/acel.13028

[208] **Exercise interactions with these supplements. See,** Gliemann L, Schmidt JF, Olesen J, et al. Resveratrol blunts the positive effects of exercise training on cardiovascular health in aged men. *J Physiol.* 2013 Aug 19

CHAPTER 24 - STEVEN KOTLER

[209] **Cost of deploying Navy SEALs based on Kotler's calculation. See,** Kotler, S., & Wheal, J. (2017). *Stealing Fire: How Silicon Valley, the Navy Seals, and Maverick Scientists Are Revolutionizing the Way We Live and Work.* New York , United States: Harper Collins, p12.

[210] **Kotler being invited to the Mind Gym. See,** Kotler & Wheal, *Stealing Fire*, p26.

[211] **The claim that Navy SEALs could reduce language acquisition from six months to six weeks. Could not find external source to prove this but assume it was anecdotal evidence from Kotler's visit to the military base. See,** Kotler & J Wheal, *Stealing Fire*, p27.

[212] **Definition of flow state. See,** Kotler & Wheal, *Stealing Fire*, p4.

[213] **Description of flow state. See,** Kotler & Wheal, *Stealing Fire*, p24.

[214] **Self-awareness of prefrontal cortex. See,** Kotler & Wheal, *Stealing Fire,* p37.

[215] **Direct quote. See,** Kotler & Wheal, *Stealing Fire,* p27.

[216] **Great overview of flow state from academic perspective. Contains evidence that flow state improves creativity. See,** Šimleša, M., Guegan, J., Blanchard, E., Tarpin-Bernard, F., & Buisine, S. (2018). The Flow Engine Framework: A Cognitive Model of Optimal Human Experience. *Europe's journal of psychology, 14*(1), 232–253. https://doi.org/10.5964/ejop.v14i1.1370

[217] **Altered states economy. See,** Kotler & Wheal, *Stealing Fire,* p30.

[218] **Study by McKinsey Consulting. See,** McKinsey Consulting. (2013, December 1). Increasing the 'meaning quotient' of work. Retrieved from https://www.mckinsey.com/business-functions/organization/our-insights/increasing-the-meaning-quotient-of-work

[219] **Not mentioned by Kotler. But alpha wave music is showing promise in increasing memory. See,** Makada, T., Ozair, D., Mohammed, M., & Abellanoza, C. (2016). Enhancing Memory Retention by Increasing Alpha and Decreasing Beta Brainwaves using Music. *Proceedings of the 9th ACM International Conference on PErvasive Technologies Related to Assistive Environments - PETRA '16.* New York, United States: ACM Press. https://doi.org/10.1145/2910674.2935851

[220] **The only study I could find that loosely supports Kotler's claim that risk increases the chance of entering the flow state. See,** Swann, C., Crust, L., Jackman, P., Vella, S. A., Allen, M. S., & Keegan, R. (2017). Psychological States Underlying Excellent Performance in Sport: Toward an Integrated Model of Flow and Clutch States. *Journal of Applied Sport Psychology, 29*(4), 375–401. https://doi.org/10.1080/10413200.2016.1272650

CHAPTER 25 – WEINSTEIN BROTHERS

[221] **The podcast where this story was first told to the public. See,** Weinstein, E., (Eric Weinstein). (2020, February 20) *Bret Weinstein on "The Portal" (w/ host Eric Weinstein), Ep. #019 - The Prediction and the DISC.* Retrieved by https://www.youtube.com/watch?v=JLb5hZLw44s&t=7424s

[222] **The term genetic hourglass to describe telomeres was borrowed from another source. See,** Foley, K., *10 years after the Nobel Prize, telomeres are still murky lead into longevity research.* (2019, December 19) Quartz. Retrieved by https://qz.com/1765469/science-is-still-studying-how-telomeres-are-linked-to-longevity/

[223] **The experiment which Greider did not cite Weinstein. See,** Hemann MT, Greider CW. Wild-derived inbred mouse strains have short telomeres. *Nucleic Acids Research*. 28: 4474-8.

[224] **Article which was published by Nature with same content as Weinstein but did not extend liability to drug industry. See,** Tyner, S.D., Venkatachalam, S., Choi, J., Jones, S., Ghebranious, N., et al., 2002. p53 *Mutant mice that display early aging-associated phenotypes*. Nature 415, 45-53.

[225] **Weinstein's original paper. See,** Weinstein, B., Ciszek, D., *The reserve-capacity hypothesis: evolutionary origins and modern implications of the trade-off between tumor-suppression and tissue-repair.* Experimental Gerontology 37 (2002) 620.

[226] **The page where Weinstein addressed Greider. See,** Weinstein, B., Ciszek, D., *The reserve-capacity hypothesis: evolutionary origins and modern implications of the trade-off between tumor-suppression and tissue-repair.* Experimental Gerontology 37 (2002) 615-627.

[227] Ibid.

[228] **Carol Greider's lecture. See,** National Human Genome Research Institute (2010, March 2) *The 2009 Jeffrey M. Trent Lecture in Cancer Research – Carol Greider.* Retrieved by https://www.youtube.com/watch?v=MpGxOR50sn4

[229] **Later Greider research which aligns with Weinstein's initial work (dates are important). See,** Feldser DM, Greider CW. Short telomeres limit tumor progression in vivo by inducing senescence. *Cancer Cell* (2007) 11: 461-9; Hao LY, Greider CW. Genomic instability in both wild-type and telomerase null MEFs. *Chromosoma* (2004) 113: 62-8.

[230] **Deaths from Vioxx. See,** Krumholz HM, Ross JS, Presler AH, Egilman DS. What have we learned from Vioxx? *BMJ*. 2007;334(7585):120-12317235089

[231] **Critique of peer review. See,** Smith R. Peer review: a flawed process at the heart of science and journals. J R Soc Med. 2006;99:178–182.

Made in the USA
Coppell, TX
18 February 2024